English Grammar Exercises: Incorrect With Answers

S0-AVN-762

1400 multiple-choice items

Daniel B. Smith

Copyright © 2022

Table of contents

Introduction

The main purpose of these book is to provide you an impressive and invaluable collection of English Grammar multiple-choice exercises with answers.

This book comprises different items and will take you on a beautiful journey towards improving your English for any exam.

There are 1400 items in this book with regard to subjects as: adjectives, adverbs, articles, conjunctions, countable and uncountable nouns, grammar, nouns, prepositions, pronouns, punctuation, verbs etc.

This book is innovative because you have to think the opposite way and choose the wrong item in the sentence.

Please keep an eye on further releases.
Good luck!⏎

Set I

1. Choose the wrong word: "Although a number of voters has cast their ballots in the city election, the supervisor of elections temporarily ended them because of a malfunction in the voting mechanism.".
    a) hast cast
    b) temporarily
    c) of

2. Choose the wrong word: "While this is not the most popular course offered at the university, just like many others classes that have low attendance in spite of their importance, at least several classes are always available.".
    a) importance
    b) others
    c) the most popular

3. Choose the wrong word: "For years, this varsity athletes have been known throughout the country for their tremendous abilities.".
    a) for
    b) tremendous
    c) this

4. Choose the wrong word: "The company had been operate in an old warehouse since its inception, when it built a huge, efficient and modern office building.".
    a) operate
    b) its
    c) efficient

5. Choose the wrong word: "Before administering the exam, the proctor required that the students take their seats and removing all items from their workplaces.".
    a) required
    b) removing
    c) their

6. Choose the wrong word: "Some people enjoy preparing their own meals while another would rather eat out regularly.".
    a) their

b) while

c) another

7. Choose the wrong word: "The news of the decision to invade with armed forces were not well received by the citizens".

    a) were

    b) to

    c) received

8. Choose the wrong word: "Air traffic controllers must use a form of communication that is universal understood because a pilot's understanding of instructions is critical.".

    a) use

    b) universal

    c) understanding

9. Choose the wrong word: "Hurricanes hardly never reach the east coast, but some that have were extremely hazardous.".

    a) never

    b) reach

    c) extremely

10. Choose the wrong word: "Children raised in foster homes requirement special attention to overcome the feelings of abandonment and isolation.".

    a) of

    b) overcome

    c) requirement

11. Choose the wrong word: "With so many choices of wireless technology, it is often difficulty to determine which offers the best value and quality.".

    a) with

    b) choices

    c) difficulty

12. Choose the wrong word: "Entering in the country in car may cause different treatment by customs officials than entering by way of mass transportation.".

    a) in

b) cause

c) entering

13. Choose the wrong word: "Some teachers enjoy writing articles and performing research, while anothers would be more content to devote all their time to teaching.".

    a) writing

    b) anothers

    c) to devote

14. Choose the wrong word: "Tests have been performed to determine whether studying TOEFL questions will help students rise their test scores.".

    a) been

    b) whether

    c) rise

15. Choose the wrong word: "The professor decided to allow the students to take the examination a second time because the low scores.".

    a) to allow

    b) because

    c) second

16. Choose the wrong word: "Having withdrawn from the race, the candidate decided supporting his opponent despite the opponent's representing the other party.".

    a) having

    b) despite

    c) supporting

17. Choose the wrong word: "The congressman, accompanied by secret service agents and aides, are preparing to enter the convention hall within the next few minutes.".

    a) are

    b) to enter

    c) within the next

18. Choose the wrong word: "Because the torrential rains that had devastated the area, the governor sent the National Guard to assist in the clean-up operation.".

    a) to assist in

b) Because

c) torrential

19. Choose the wrong word: "Lack of sanitation in restaurants are a major cause of disease in some areas of the country.".

    a) of sanitation

    b) cause of

    c) are

20. Choose the wrong word: "Had the committee members considered the alternatives more carefully, they would have realized that the second was better as the first.".

    a) more carefully

    b) as the first

    c) second was

21. Choose the wrong word: "Malnutrition is a major cause of death in those countries where the cultivation of rice have been impeded by recurrent drought.".

    a) is a major

    b) have

    c) in those countries

22. Choose the wrong word: "The decision to withdraw all support from the activities of the athletes are causing an uproar among the athletes' fans.".

    a) among

    b) to withdraw

    c) are causing

23. Choose the wrong word: "Underutilized species of fish has been proposed as a solution to the famine in many underdeveloped countries.".

    a) has been

    b) as

    c) to the famine

24. Choose the wrong word: "Because the residents had worked so diligent to renovate the old building, the manager had a party.".

    a) had worked

    b) diligent

    c) to renovate

25. Choose the wrong word: "David's wisdom teeth were troubling him, so he went to a dental surgeon to see about having them pull.".
    a) them pull
    b) were troubling
    c) to see

26. Choose the wrong word: "Sarah had better to change her study habits if she hopes to be admitted to a good university.".
    a) had
    b) to a good university
    c) to change

27. Choose the wrong word: "Overeating, in addition to lack of attention to nutrition, are said to be the major cause of obesity in the United States.".
    a) lack
    b) are
    c) cause

28. Choose the wrong word: "Because the students showed they had read the materials so thorough, the instructor decided not to administer an exam.".
    a) thorough
    b) because
    c) to administer

29. Choose the wrong word: "Sarah decided to wait until after she had taken her exams before having her wisdom teeth pull.".
    a) to wait
    b) having
    c) pull

30. Choose the wrong word: "Hardly the plane had landed when Daniel realized that he had left the file that he needed at his office.".
    a) Hardly the plane had
    b) realized
    c) that he had

31. Choose the wrong word: "The consultant said management had better to formalize its employment policies and procedures in order to avoid adverse employment claims in the future.".

a) avoid

b) to formalize

c) adverse

32. Choose the wrong word: "The author has not rarely written anything that was not a best-seller.".

a) author

b) anything

c) not rarely

33. Choose the wrong word: "The Dean of The College of Education has already to decide whether to permit the meeting to be held on campus.".

a) already to decide

b) the

c) to permit

34. Choose the wrong word: "The professor had already completed calculation of the final grades and had submit them to the office when Mary delivered her paper.".

a) already

b) of

c) had submit

35. Choose the wrong word: "Several cars plunged into the water when the pier was striking by a barge that separated from its tugboat.".

a) from

b) was striking

c) plunged

36. Choose the wrong word: "The new prospect for the team has great height and agility, but the coaches do not believe he moves enough quickly to play in the position that they need to fill.".

a) play

b) enough quickly

c) height

37. Choose the wrong word: "So much people applied for service from the new company that it found it impossible to meet the demand.".

a) for

b) much

c) impossible

38. Choose the wrong word: "The meeting is being held in the fifth floor of the convention center, but there are functions on every floor.".
    a) in
    b) being
    c) are

39. Choose the wrong word: "An orangutan escaped from the zoo and was foraged food in a residential neighborhood.".
    a) in
    b) residential
    c) was foraged

40. Choose the wrong word: "The school officials are considering a comprehensive planning to alleviate the problem of overcrowding in the dormitories.".
    a) planning
    b) alleviate
    c) are

41. Choose the wrong word: "Spanish is the only course that it is not offered in the summer term, but there are several classes offered in the fall.".
    a) offered
    b) it
    c) several

42. Choose the wrong word: "Sarah was not best speaker in the class, but her personality and ability to convey her feelings helped her become the most requested.".
    a) not best
    b) her
    c) requested

43. Choose the wrong word: "The issues learned during the early stages of the project causing the researchers to initiate additional research.".
    a) during
    b) additional
    c) causing

44. Choose the wrong word: "Only when black bear has been spotted by the forest rangers will this portion of the park be closed down.".

a) when black

b) will

c) closed

45. Choose the wrong word: "Television news producers are sometimes accuse of sensationalism, but it appears that is what the public desires.".

    a) news

    b) what

    c) accuse

46. Choose the wrong word: "The workers attempted to free the cat from the trap, but several obstacles were in way.".

    a) free

    b) in way

    c) attempted

47. Choose the wrong word: "Not only could the younger people completed all the work quickly and accurately, but the retired workers could also.".

    a) completed

    b) could

    c) also

48. Choose the wrong word: "He's not having finished his thesis did not discourage him from applying for other degree program.".

    a) finished

    b) discourage

    c) other

49. Choose the wrong word: "That investors in the stock market enjoys increases and suffer declines is simply a fact of the financial market, and a smart investor is not too excited about the former or crestfallen about the latter.".

    a) former

    b) declines

    c) enjoys

50. Choose the wrong word: "Having been found guilty of racketeering, even though he was never proven guilty of many crimes he was believe to have committed, the mobster was sentenced to a number of years in prison.".

a) proven

b) believe

c) have

51. Choose the wrong word: "Had Daniel be able to complete his thesis instead of returning to work, he would have graduated a year ago.".

a) be

b) complete

c) have

52. Choose the wrong word: "After the data has received and reviewed, the finance department employees should be able to determine the best course of action.".

a) be

b) to determine

c) has received

53. Choose the wrong word: "Owing a home, the dream of many, an unattainable goal for many young people without aid from governmental and non-profit sources.".

a) an

b) aid

c) sources

54. Choose the wrong word: "After the jury had determined liability, its next task was to decide how much money should it assess as damages.".

a) next

b) should it

c) to decide

55. Choose the wrong word: "If the Board had not reversed its position on the petition to approve the fence, the owner would had to remove it.".

a) remove

b) its

c) would had

56. Choose the wrong word: "A prolific writer, even when he was teaching a number of classes, Daniel Smith never achieving popularity among the masses.".

a) was

b) achieving

c) classes

57. Choose the wrong word: "Attorneys who practice in the area of personal injury generally spending considerably more money on advertising in telephone books and on television than other types of attorneys.".

    a) other

    b) spending

    c) types

58. Choose the wrong word: "This city, known as oldest city in the country is home to the oldest schoolhouse.".

    a) city

    b) the country

    c) as oldest

59. Choose the wrong word: "The committee voted purchase the land next to the company's existing building, but the resolution was not approved at the full Board meeting.".

    a) voted purchase

    b) next

    c) existing

60. Choose the wrong word: "Students may buy used books if they had been readily available and correctly priced.".

    a) readily

    b) used

    c) had been

61. Choose the wrong word: "Without a doubt, the best way to do well in college to keep up constantly with the homework, read everything that is required and regularly outline all the class notes.".

    a) regularly

    b) doubt

    c) way to

62. Choose the wrong word: "In the early morning, the hikers broke camp and began the long trek towards home, hoping to before noon arrive.".

    a) before noon arrive

b) towards

c) began

63. Choose the wrong word: "Though the danger had passed, officials were hesitant to allow residents to return to their homes because they were unsure how much damage caused by the high winds.".

    a) hesitant

    b) caused

    c) to return

64. Choose the wrong word: "Daniel is certain to be hired for the position because at his interview he displayed his talents in writing, speaking, organizing, delegating and to lead.".

    a) position

    b) because

    c) to lead

65. Choose the wrong word: "Hepatitis C generally occurs 20 to 30 year after one is exposed to the illness.".

    a) year

    b) exposed

    c) occurs

66. Choose the wrong word: "The knee is the recipient of constant pressure, which causes them to fail often and requires replacement with artificial parts.".

    a) recipient

    b) them

    c) to fail

67. Choose the wrong word: "Effective speaking and proficient writing is generally seen as requirements for a professor to achieve tenure.".

    a) speaking

    b) proficient

    c) is

68. Choose the wrong word: "Universities often ignore a student's lack of scholastically ability when the student has great athletic potential in a sport that is important to the school.".

    a) lack

b) athletic

c) scholastically

69. Choose the wrong word: "Daniel Smith he wrote down-to-earth accounts of individuals and families who suffered through the Great Depression.".

    a) individuals

    b) he wrote

    c) accounts

70. Choose the wrong word: "Numismatics, the study of coins, can be very rewarding once a person becomes familiar with determining the date and type of a coin, as well as grade it.".

    a) grade

    b) once

    c) familiar

71. Choose the wrong word: "Listening to recorded books while driving is a means of utilize time wisely.".

    a) means

    b) recorded

    c) utilize

72. Choose the wrong word: "The passionate and exuberant display of the orchestra conductor moving several members of the audience to tears.".

    a) of

    b) audience

    c) moving

73. Choose the wrong word: "In 1947, he became a first Black American to play major league baseball.".

    a) to play

    b) a

    c) in

74. Choose the wrong word: "As a company grows in size, it is important to maintain communicate among the various departments.".

    a) communicate

    b) in

    c) as

75. Choose the wrong word: "Research involving animals is useful when researchers developing medicines to combat illnesses of both animals and people.".

    a) involving

    b) to combat

    c) when

76. Choose the wrong word: "Rocks can be broken apart by water that seeps into the cracks and freeze in low temperatures.".

    a) broken apart

    b) that

    c) freeze

77. Choose the wrong word: "This city, the capital of the state, are not only the largest city in the country but also a typical metropolitan area, often used in market research.".

    a) but also

    b) are

    c) used

78. Choose the wrong word: "Although maple trees are among the most colorful varieties in the fall, they lose its leaves sooner than oak trees.".

    a) its

    b) among

    c) in the fall

79. Choose the wrong word: "The teacher told the students to don't discuss the take-home exam with each other.".

    a) discuss

    b) with each other

    c) to don't

80. Choose the wrong word: "Because she didn't like shop very much, she did most of it with her personal computer.".

    a) did

    b) shop

    c) with

81. Choose the wrong word: "Knowledges about cultures provides insights into the learned behaviors of groups.".

    a) learned

b) knowledges

c) insights into

82. Choose the wrong word: "Some people think that the desire to wear sunglasses are more a need to impress than to protect the eyes.".

    a) that

    b) than to

    c) are

83. Choose the wrong word: "Those of us who have a family history of heart disease should make yearly appointments with their doctors.".

    a) their

    b) should make

    c) yearly

84. Choose the wrong word: "If he would have lived a little longer, he probably would have won the election.".

    a) a little longer

    b) probably

    c) would have lived

85. Choose the wrong word: "Excavations in several mounds and villages on the east bank of the Euphrates River have revealed a new city, an ancient community that had been laying under later reconstructions of the city of Babylon.".

    a) on the east bank

    b) had been laying

    c) later

86. Choose the wrong word: "Aluminum has a hard imperious coasting which protects the metal from corrode.".

    a) corrode

    b) hard

    c) imperious

87. Choose the wrong word: "After learned to print, elementary school children learn cursive writing.".

    a) children

    b) writing

    c) learned

88. Choose the wrong word: "Studies of job satisfaction are unreliable because there is so many variables and because the admission of dissatisfaction may be viewed as a personal failure.".

    a) many

    b) because

    c) is

89. Choose the wrong word: "Computers have made access to information instantly available just by push a few buttons.".

    a) have

    b) by push

    c) instantly available

90. Choose the wrong word: "Latex rubber is made from a milky substantial in plants and trees of the sapodilla family.".

    a) substantial

    b) milky

    c) tress of

91. Choose the wrong word: "Fishing have been found to contain a particular type of fat that may help lower blood cholesterol levels.".

    a) levels

    b) to contain

    c) Fishing

92. Choose the wrong word: "When caterpillars are fully-grown, they attach themselves to a leave or twig and form a shell around itself called a cocoon.".

    a) around itself

    b) are fully-grown

    c) called

93. Choose the wrong word: "In experiments with large numbers of animals crowded in small cages, some have not been affected, but the rest of have shown all of the symptoms associated with stress and mental illness.".

    a) large numbers

    b) the rest of

    c) have shown

94. Choose the wrong word: "The athlete, together with his coach and several relatives, are traveling to the competition.".

    a) his coach

    b) with

    c) are

95. Choose the wrong word: "The man earned the funds to go west by sale his new ideas about growing potatoes.".

    a) sale

    b) the funds

    c) about

96. Choose the wrong word: "Before television became so popular, Americans used to entertain each other in the evening by playing games, saying stories and singing songs.".

    a) so popular

    b) saying

    c) each other

97. Choose the wrong word: "The professor had already given the homework assignment when he had remembered that Monday was a holiday.".

    a) Monday

    b) was

    c) had remembered

98. Choose the wrong word: "Alice Wilson, she spent her life working with the health and welfare of the families of workers.".

    a) she

    b) her life

    c) welfare

99. Choose the wrong word: "It is extremely important for an engineer to know to use a computer.".

    a) it is

    b) to know

    c) extremely

100. Choose the wrong word: "The master of ceremonies announced in a loud and clear voice and told that the dinner would be late due to unforeseen circumstances.".

a) of ceremonies

b) due to

c) and told

101. Choose the wrong word: "Narcis, a character in mythology, gazed at his own image in a pool so ardently that he fell into itself and downed.".

    a) into itself

    b) his own

    c) that

102. Choose the wrong word: "The professor was considering postponing the examination until the following week because the student's confusion.".

    a) considering

    b) because

    c) the following week

103. Choose the wrong word: "Sinaitic is the name of an alphabet which developed their symbols from Egyptian hieroglyphics.".

    a) symbols

    b) which developed

    c) their

104. Choose the wrong word: "The native people in the Americas were referred to as Indians because, according to the believe at the time, Columbus had reached the East Indies.".

    a) believe

    b) referred to

    c) had reached

105. Choose the wrong word: "After to have won the light-heavyweight title at the 1968 Olympic Games, he began to box professionally.".

    a) began

    b) to have

    c) professionally

106. Choose the wrong word: "There are many different ways of comparing the economy of one nation with those of another.".

    a) another

    b) of comparing

    c) those

107. Choose the wrong word: "He said he must come to the party if he finishes his assignment for next week's seminar.".

    a) must come

    b) finishes

    c) for

108. Choose the wrong word: "The basic law of addition, subtraction, multiplication and division are taught to all elementary school students.".

    a) division

    b) taught

    c) law

109. Choose the wrong word: "She has not rarely missed a play or concert since she was seventeen years old.".

    a) a play

    b) not rarely

    c) since

110. Choose the wrong word: "The need for a well-rounded education was an idea espoused by the Greeks in time of Socrates.".

    a) in time of

    b) for

    c) espoused

111. Choose the wrong word: "To assure the safety of those workers who must handle radioactive material, the employer should not leave them enter contaminated areas without protective clothing.".

    a) to assure

    b) leave

    c) who

112. Choose the wrong word: "The religion attempts to clarify man's relationship with a superhuman power.".

    a) The religion

    b) to clarify

    c) man's

113. Choose the wrong word: "In 1985, according to the National Center for Health Statistics, the average life expectancy for people born during that year is 75 years.".

    a) during

b) born

c) is

114. Choose the wrong word: "Many of the famous advertising offices are located in Matrix Avenue.".

    a) in

    b) located

    c) many

115. Choose the wrong word: "When he took the ticket out of from his pocket, a hundred dollar bill fell to the floor without his noticing it.".

    a) without

    b) from his pocket

    c) to

116. Choose the wrong word: "Each of the nurses report to the operating room when his or her name is called.".

    a) of the

    b) his or her name

    c) report

117. Choose the wrong word: "Because blood from various individuals may different in the type of antigen on the surface of the red cells, a dangerous reaction can occur between the donor and recipient in a blood transfusion.".

    a) and

    b) because

    c) different

118. Choose the wrong word: "Both viruses also genes are made from nucleoproteins, the essential chemicals with which living matter duplicates itself.".

    a) also

    b) living

    c) are

119. Choose the wrong word: "Although the Red Cross accepts blood from most donors, the nurses will not leave you give blood if you have just had a cold.".

    a) accepts

b) leave

c) had

120. Choose the wrong word: "Economists have tried to discourage the use of this phrase and encouraging the more accurate phrase "developing nation" in order to suggest an ongoing process.".

    a) the use

    b) the more

    c) encouraging

121. Choose the wrong word: "Since infection can cause both fever as well as pain, it is a good idea to check a patient's temperature.".

    a) can cause

    b) as well as

    c) to check

122. Choose the wrong word: "Nuclear powers production in the US is controlled by the Nuclear Regulatory Commission.".

    a) the

    b) is

    c) powers

123. Choose the wrong word: "The intent of the Historical Society is to restore old buildings and the increase of interest in the history of the area.".

    a) the increase of

    b) is

    c) area

124. Choose the wrong word: "The volume four of our encyclopedia set has been missing for two months.".

    a) has been missing

    b) for

    c) The volume

125. Choose the wrong word: "Professor Smith teaches both anthropology as well as sociology each fall.".

    a) teaches

    b) both

    c) anthropology

126. Choose the wrong word: "Because helicopters are capable of hovering in midair, they are particularly useful for rescue missions, military operates and transportation.".

    a) particularly

    b) operates

    c) of hovering

127. Choose the wrong word: "All of we students must have an identification card in order to check books out of the library.".

    a) of

    b) out

    c) we

128. Choose the wrong word: "Sometime several nations become partners in a larger political state, as for example, the four nations joined in the UK.".

    a) several nations

    b) become

    c) Sometime

129. Choose the wrong word: "The Gray Wolf, a species reintroduced into their native habitat in National Park, has begun to breed naturally there.".

    a) their native habitat

    b) has begun

    c) reintroduced

130. Choose the wrong word: "Major advertising companies have traditionally volunteered its time to public service accounts.".

    a) to public

    b) its

    c) advertising

131. Choose the wrong word: "Coconut oil produces a soap whom will lather in salt water as well as fresh.".

    a) whom

    b) salt water

    c) produces

132. Choose the wrong word: "The organizers of the charity were more than surprised at how many people lined up to receive the clothes donating by the outgoing mayor.".

a) how many

b) the outgoing

c) donating

133. Choose the wrong word: "Until recently women were forbidden by law from owning property.".

a) were

b) by law

c) from owning

134. Choose the wrong word: "He has become one of the greatest dancer that the ballet world has ever known.".

a) has become

b) dancer

c) ever known

135. Choose the wrong word: "Tea did not become popular in Europe until the mid 17th century when it has been first imported to England and Holland.".

a) first

b) did not become

c) has been

136. Choose the wrong word: "During wedding ceremonies in the United States guests are usually silence.".

a) During

b) ceremonies

c) silence

137. Choose the wrong word: "Supersonic transport such the Concorde will probably be widely accepted as soon as problems of noise and atmospheric pollution are resolved.".

a) such

b) widely

c) as soon

138. Choose the wrong word: "Some religions have none deity but are philosophies that function instead of religions.".

a) none

b) have

c) instead of religions

139. Choose the wrong word: "A vine climbs from one tree to another, continuing to grow and support itself even when the original supporting tree is not longer alive.".

    a) to grow

    b) supporting

    c) not longer

140. Choose the wrong word: "Every candidate under considering for a federal job must undergo a thorough medical examination.".

    a) considering

    b) undergo

    c) medical

141. Choose the wrong word: "He achieved world recognition as both a dancer as well as a choreographer.".

    a) as well as

    b) a dancer

    c) achieved

142. Choose the wrong word: "In a corporation the approval of a majority of stockholders may be required before a major decision can be done.".

    a) a major

    b) approval

    c) done

143. Choose the wrong word: "A fiber-optic cable across the Pacific went into service in April 1990 link the US and Japan.".

    a) across

    b) link

    c) in

144. Choose the wrong word: "A good artist like a good engineer learns as much from their mistakes as from successes.".

    a) like

    b) from

    c) their

145. Choose the wrong word: "Almost all life depends to chemical reactions with oxygen to produce energy.".

    a) depends to

b) to produce

c) almost all

146. Choose the wrong word: "If a rash occurs within twenty-four hours after taking a new medication, the treatment should discontinued.".

    a) after taking

    b) medication

    c) should discontinued

147. Choose the wrong word: "When one experiences a change in diet by, for example, moving to a new location, you may also experience temporary problems with the digestive tract.".

    a) moving

    b) experience

    c) you

148. Choose the wrong word: "The process of making Egyptian sun-dried mud brick are much the same today as it was in prehistoric times.".

    a) of making

    b) are much

    c) as it

149. Choose the wrong word: "The best way to eliminate a pest is to controlling the food accessible to it.".

    a) to controlling

    b) The best

    c) food accessible

150. Choose the wrong word: "The professor told him to write a short but it must be comprehensive paper about the experiment.".

    a) comprehensive

    b) it must be

    c) him

151. Choose the wrong word: "Mumps are a very common disease which usually affects children.".

    a) which

    b) common disease

    c) are

152. Choose the wrong word: "The symptoms of diabetes in the early stages are too slight that people don't notice them.".

a) them

b) symptoms

c) too

153. Choose the wrong word: "We know that in 1000 A.D. this man landed on the North American coast, and that him and his Norwegian companions were the first white men to see the New World.".

a) him

b) were

c) to see

154. Choose the wrong word: "Hyde Park sets on top of a bluff overlooking the Hudson River.".

a) overlooking

b) sets

c) the Hudson River

155. Choose the wrong word: "After he had ran for half a mile, he passed the stick to the next runner.".

a) for

b) the next

c) had ran

156. Choose the wrong word: "Although business practices have been applied successfully to agriculture, farming is different other industries.".

a) different

b) farming

c) applied

157. Choose the wrong word: "Although there are exceptions, as whole, the male of the bird species is more brilliantly colored.".

a) there are

b) as whole

c) brilliantly

158. Choose the wrong word: "In the US, the bark the eastern hemlock is the main source of tannin for curing leather.".

a) the main

b) source

c) bark the

159. Choose the wrong word: "Authors Samuel Morison won two prizes, one in 1943 for a biography and the other in 1960 for another biography.".
      a) won
      b) the other
      c) Authors

160. Choose the wrong word: "When zippers are easy to use, it took almost half a century to perfect the zipper and find a way to manufacture them economically.".
      a) it took
      b) When zippers
      c) them

161. Choose the wrong word: "The Augustinian monk performed many experiments which have won him the title of "Father of Genetic".
      a) performed
      b) have won
      c) which

162. Choose the wrong word: "Some gorillas beat their chests as an express of high spirits.".
      a) express
      b) beat
      c) high

163. Choose the wrong word: "After the police had tried unsuccessfully to determine to who the car belonged, they towed it into the station.".
      a) the police
      b) unsuccessfully
      c) who

164. Choose the wrong word: "The town we visited was a four-days journey from our hotel, so we took the train instead of the bus.".
      a) was
      b) of the bus
      c) four-days

165. Choose the wrong word: "As soon as they arrived at the hotel they took the elevator to their room and straight to bed because they were so tired.".
      a) took

b) straight to bed

c) as soon as

166. Choose the wrong word: "One of the primary cause of accidents in coal mines is the accumulation of gas.".

    a) cause

    b) coal mines

    c) gas

167. Choose the wrong word: "Before becoming successful, the former vice president of General Motors was so poor that he has to use the hayloft of a barn as a laboratory.".

    a) as

    b) so poor

    c) has to

168. Choose the wrong word: "The senior student was not able to find out why the experiment failed, and neither his professor could.".

    a) out

    b) could

    c) not able

169. Choose the wrong word: "On the 19th century frontier, school, along with the church and the jail, was a key public building in the community.".

    a) school

    b) the church

    c) a key

170. Choose the wrong word: "The water in the Great Salt Lake is at less four times saltier than seawater.".

    a) than

    b) saltier

    c) at less

171. Choose the wrong word: "The theory of natural selection is used to explain which animals of a species will die prematurely and which will survival.".

    a) is used

    b) which

    c) survival

172. Choose the wrong word: "The yard sales are a good way to get rid of all those things that have been cluttering up our garages and attics for years.".

    a) The yard sales

    b) that

    c) been

173. Choose the wrong word: "Traveling ballet companies were uncommon before her Augusta Smith formed the first traveling troupe.".

    a) traveling

    b) were

    c) her

174. Choose the wrong word: "To improvement the stability of the building, a concrete foundation two feet thick must be installed.".

    a) feet

    b) improvement

    c) stability

175. Choose the wrong word: "Aristotle, the famous Greek philosopher, believed that the brain was an organ that cooled a heart.".

    a) the famous

    b) an organ

    c) a heart

176. Choose the wrong word: "The Fairness Doctrine of the FCC requires that radio and television stations give equal time to opposing sides of issues controversial.".

    a) issues controversial

    b) stations

    c) requires that

177. Choose the wrong word: "Together they wrote nine musicals, the first of whose was this one.".

    a) Together

    b) whose

    c) first

178. Choose the wrong word: "Benjamin was the editor of the largest newspaper in the colonies, a diplomatic representative to France and later to England, and he invented many useful devices.".

a) the largest

b) he invented

c) many

179. Choose the wrong word: "Agronomists study crop disease, selective breeding, crop rotation and climatic factors, as well soil content and erosion.".

a) as well

b) crop disease

c) and

180. Choose the wrong word: "Despite its smaller size, the Indian Ocean is as deep the Atlantic Ocean.".

a) smaller size

b) its

c) as deep

181. Choose the wrong word: "What happened in New York were a reaction from city workers, including firemen and policemen who had been laid off from their jobs.".

a) were

b) including

c) their

182. Choose the wrong word: "Economic goods often consist to material items, but they can also be services to people.".

a) goods

b) be

c) to

183. Choose the wrong word: "It is essential that vitamins are supplied either by foods or by supplementary tablets for normal growth to occur.".

a) to occur

b) are

c) by supplementary tablets

184. Choose the wrong word: "Although there are new drugs on the market, deaths from malaria are being increasing in some parts of the world.".

a) are being increasing

b) Although

c) in some parts

185. Choose the wrong word: "Melanin, a pigment that lays under the skin, is responsible for skin color, including the variations that occur among different races.".

    a) lays

    b) is

    c) among

186. Choose the wrong word: "With a policy of eminent domain, the state has control ultimate of all real property.".

    a) control ultimate

    b) real

    c) policy

187. Choose the wrong word: "Representative democracy seemed evolve simultaneously during the eighteenth and nineteenth centuries in Britain, Europe and the United States.".

    a) during

    b) simultaneously

    c) evolve

188. Choose the wrong word: "If the oxygen supply in the atmosphere was not replenished by plants, it would soon be exhausted.".

    a) be exhausted

    b) by plants

    c) in the atmosphere

189. Choose the wrong word: "For photosynthesis to occur, a leaf requires carbon dioxide, water and light is also necessary.".

    a) requires

    b) to occur

    c) light is also necessary

190. Choose the wrong word: "Although the Indians had lived for centuries in the US, when the European settlers came in the seventeenth century, the newcomers began a systematic effort to push them further into the wilderness.".

    a) to push

b) their

c) in the seventeenth

191. Choose the wrong word: "If the ozone gases of the atmosphere did not filter out the ultraviolet rays of the sun, life, as we know it, would not have evolved on earth.".

    a) on earth

    b) as

    c) did not filter out

192. Choose the wrong word: "It is not surprised that the Arabs, who possessed a remarkable gift for astronomy, mathematics and geometry, were also skillful mapmakers.".

    a) surprised

    b) possessed

    c) were

193. Choose the wrong word: "Albert Einstein was such brilliant a scientist that many of his colleagues had to study for several years in order to form opinions about his theories.".

    a) study

    b) such brilliant a scientist

    c) many of his colleagues

194. Choose the wrong word: "A one hundred-horsepower tractor can make the work of a large number of horses.".

    a) a large number

    b) can

    c) make

195. Choose the wrong word: "Ships are able to move through canals because locks, rectangular areas with varying water levels.".

    a) varying

    b) because locks

    c) to move through

196. Choose the wrong word: "Diamond itself is the only material hard enough to cut and polishes diamonds.".

    a) polishes

    b) hard enough

    c) itself

197. Choose the wrong word: "The tornado uprooted all the power lines leading to the town so the inhabitants had to live in darkness until new ones.".

    a) leading

    b) had to

    c) until new ones

198. Choose the wrong word: "Before the nineteenth century it was rarely to find organized systems of adult education.".

    a) systems

    b) Before

    c) rarely

199. Choose the wrong word: "This new model not only saves time but also energy by operating on two batteries instead of four.".

    a) This

    b) energy

    c) operating

200. Choose the wrong word: "When scientists discovered how soap works, it became possible to do synthetic detergents out of petroleum.".

    a) to do

    b) discovered

    c) how

201. Choose the wrong word: "When Daniel visited Alaska, he lived in a igloo in the winter months as well as in the spring.".

    a) months

    b) a

    c) lived

202. Choose the wrong word: "The price of gold depends in several factors, including supply and demand in relation to the value of the dollar.".

    a) several factors

    b) in relation to

    c) depends in

203. Choose the wrong word: "There are many ways to preserve fruit, for example freezing, canning and to dry.".

    a) There are

b) to dry

c) fruit

204. Choose the wrong word: "We were taught that one's future is entirely in our own hands and neither a matter of family connections nor of fate and good luck.".

    a) one's

    b) were taught

    c) own hands

205. Choose the wrong word: "Work is often measure in units called foot pounds.".

    a) work

    b) is

    c) measure

206. Choose the wrong word: "Archaeological evidence reveals that Native Americans lived on the East Coast of the US 13 centuries before.".

    a) before

    b) reveals that

    c) of the

207. Choose the wrong word: "Exercising well is as important to your health as sleep and eating correctly.".

    a) correctly

    b) sleep

    c) eating

208. Choose the wrong word: "The mayor and the council, meeting at the city hall as usual, they did not discuss the proposed new sports complex as planned.".

    a) planned

    b) they did not

    c) meeting

209. Choose the wrong word: "Linoleum is a trade name for the waterproof floors covering most often used in kitchens.".

    a) floors

    b) trade

    c) most often

210. Choose the wrong word: "The planning committee told Sarah that they had decided hers proposal would be adopted.".

    a) planning

    b) had decided

    c) hers

211. Choose the wrong word: "Because there were so few women in the early Western states, the freedom and rights of Western women were more extensive than Eastern ladies.".

    a) more extensive

    b) so few women

    c) than Eastern ladies

212. Choose the wrong word: "It has been found that the length of light or dark periods influence certain activities of flowering plants.".

    a) certain activities

    b) of flowering plants

    c) influence

213. Choose the wrong word: "Unless one subscribes to a large metropolitan newspaper such as the WSJ or WP, one will find very few news from abroad.".

    a) few news

    b) such as

    c) one

214. Choose the wrong word: "The masterpiece "A Christmas Carol" wrote by Dickens in 1843.".

    a) The

    b) wrote

    c) by

215. Choose the wrong word: "Many of the characters portrayed by writer Carol Oates is mentally ill.".

    a) portrayed

    b) mentally

    c) is

216. Choose the wrong word: "Daniel Smith, a famous climber India, learned the basics of his sport on the steep cliffs hanging over a rocky bay near his home.".

a) learned

b) a famous climber India

c) basics

217. Choose the wrong word: "International trade, going traveling, and television have lain the groundwork for modern global life styles.".

a) going traveling

b) have lain

c) for

218. Choose the wrong word: "Astronomers do not know how many galaxies there are, but is it thought that there are millions or perhaps billions.".

a) there are

b) how many

c) is it

219. Choose the wrong word: "Alfalfa is a nutritious crop rich in proteins, minerals and with vitamins.".

a) rich in

b) with vitamins

c) nutritious

220. Choose the wrong word: "Even a professional psychologist may have difficulty talking calm and logically about his own problems.".

a) calm

b) about

c) even

221. Choose the wrong word: "A largely percentage of Canadian export business is with the United States.".

a) with

b) of

c) largely

222. Choose the wrong word: "While his racing days, the man earned a record $7.5 million, $2.1 million more than his closest competitor.".

a) earned

b) While

c) closest

223. Choose the wrong word: "Before we returned from swimming in the river near the camp, someone had stole our clothes, and we had to walk back with our towels around us.".

    a) had stole

    b) Before we returned

    c) back

224. Choose the wrong word: "The girls were sorry to had missed the singers when they arrived at the airport.".

    a) were sorry

    b) when

    c) had missed

225. Choose the wrong word: "May Alcott infused her own life into the character of Jo in book "Little Women".".

    a) book

    b) into

    c) of

226. Choose the wrong word: "Daniel has called his lawyer last to tell him about his problems, but was told that the lawyer had gone to a lecture.".

    a) had gone

    b) has called

    c) to tell

227. Choose the wrong word: "The indiscriminate and continual use of any drug without medical supervision can be danger".

    a) without

    b) danger

    c) use of

228. Choose the wrong word: "The idea that artistic achievement rank in importance with scientific achievements has been upheld by painters, writers, and musicals for centuries.".

    a) rank

    b) upheld

    c) musicals

229. Choose the wrong word: "Without alphabetical order, dictionaries would be impossibility to use.".

    a) dictionaries

b) impossibility

c) to use

230. Choose the wrong word: "Americans annually import more than $2 billion worthy of Italian clothing, jewelry and shoes.".

a) worthy

b) more

c) clothing

231. Choose the wrong word: "The results of the test proved to Brian and me that needed to study harder and watch less movies on television if we wanted to receive scholarships.".

a) me

b) to

c) less

232. Choose the wrong word: "In the sixteenth century a French mathematician used some vowels to represent a unknown number.".

a) a

b) to represent

c) sixteenth century

233. Choose the wrong word: "The explanation that our instructor gave us was different than the one yours gave you.".

a) our

b) than

c) gave us

234. Choose the wrong word: "The bell signaling the end of the first period rang loud, interrupting the professor's closing comment's.".

a) signaling

b) interrupting

c) loud

235. Choose the wrong word: "Anyone reproducing copyrighted works without permission of the holders of the copyrights are breaking the law.".

a) are

b) reproducing

c) breaking

236. Choose the wrong word: "The historian reported that one hundred thousand men are employed for twenty years to build the Great Pyramid

at Gizeh.".

    a) to build

    b) are

    c) for

237. Choose the wrong word: "The patient who was not supposed to be released until the end of the week was told to dress in clothes and report to the nurses' station.".

    a) until

    b) the nurses' station

    c) in clothes

238. Choose the wrong word: "The corals can be divided into three groups, two of which is extinct.".

    a) can be divided

    b) of which

    c) is

239. Choose the wrong word: "The leader emphasized the need for justice and equality between his people.".

    a) for justice

    b) between

    c) the need

240. Choose the wrong word: "Industrialist Henry Ford introduced assembly-line techniques into the manufacturer of motor vehicles.".

    a) manufacturer

    b) industrialist

    c) vehicles

241. Choose the wrong word: "The soil is composed of a mixture of organic matter called humus and inorganic matter derived from rocks.".

    a) called

    b) The soil

    c) is

242. Choose the wrong word: "The term Neanderthal was used to describe widely dispersed populations that lived between 100,000 and 30,000 years ago.".

    a) lived

b) that

c) was used

243. Choose the wrong word: "It has been preserve as a national historic monument because it was the site of a major Civil War battle in which many lives were lost.".

    a) because

    b) were lost

    c) preserve

244. Choose the wrong word: "That one a talented child actress, Shirley Black has established herself as a career diplomat, serving both as a representative in the United Nations and as an ambassador abroad.".

    a) serving

    b) That once

    c) herself

245. Choose the wrong word: "Some of us have to study their lessons more carefully if we expect to pass this examination.".

    a) their

    b) have to

    c) to pass

246. Choose the wrong word: "John Dewey thought that children will learn better through participating in experiences rather than through listening to lecture.".

    a) will learn

    b) better

    c) rather than

247. Choose the wrong word: "Overseas telephone service has been expanding fastly since its inauguration in 1927.".

    a) expanding

    b) fastly

    c) in 1927

248. Choose the wrong word: "Historically there has been only two major factions in the Republican Party – the liberals and the conservatives.".

    a) only

    b) there

    c) has been

249. Choose the wrong word: "Computers, who keep constant track of inventories and handle all billing, have become the backbone of the large business firms.".

   a) constant
   b) who
   c) track

250. Choose the wrong word: "The ozone layer must be protected because it shields the Earth from excessive ultraviolet radiations.".

   a) radiations
   b) must be protected
   c) it

251. Choose the wrong word: "Papyrus was used for to make not only paper but also sails, baskets and clothing.".

   a) for to make
   b) was used
   c) and

252. Choose the wrong word: "Much Civil War battles were fought in Virginia than in other state.".

   a) other
   b) state
   c) Much

253. Choose the wrong word: "Migraines were usually worse than tension headaches and can be so intense as to cause vomiting and vision problems.".

   a) to cause
   b) were usually
   c) vomiting

254. Choose the wrong word: "Before he starting work on the excavation the archaeologist decided to study the maps in the local museum first.".

   a) he starting
   b) the
   c) first

255. Choose the wrong word: "Despite of rain or snow there are always more than fifty thousand fans at their football games.".

   a) than

b) there are

c) Despite of

256. Choose the wrong word: "The amount of women earning Master's Degrees has risen sharply in recent years.".

    a) has risen

    b) The amount of

    c) recent years

257. Choose the wrong word: "When the temperature is risen to burning point without a source of escape for the heat, spontaneous combustion occurs.".

    a) risen

    b) for the heat

    c) the burning point

258. Choose the wrong word: "When he was a little boy, Mark would walk along the piers, watch the river boats, swimming and fish in the Mississippi.".

    a) would walk

    b) watch

    c) swimming

259. Choose the wrong word: "The influence of the nation's literature, art and science have captured widespread attention.".

    a) science

    b) have

    c) widespread

260. Choose the wrong word: "She wrote and productioned her first play while she was in high school.".

    a) productioned

    b) play

    c) wrote

261. Choose the wrong word: "A liter is one of the metric measurements, aren't they?".

    a) one of the

    b) measurements

    c) aren't they

262. Choose the wrong word: "The most visible remind of the close relationship between the United States and France is the famous Statue of Liberty, which stands in New York harbor.".

    a) remind

    b) between

    c) which

263. Choose the wrong word: "A five-thousand-dollars reward was offered for the capture of the escaped criminals.".

    a) was offered

    b) for the capture

    c) dollars

264. Choose the wrong word: "In the dry season any fishes burrow in the mud and hibernate in a large mud cocoon.".

    a) the mud

    b) any fishes

    c) the dry

265. Choose the wrong word: "Pollution, which affects nearly all countries, increase the risk of disease as well as harming the environment.".

    a) which affects

    b) increase

    c) harming the environment

266. Choose the wrong word: "Did they tell you that has in our town an excellent beach less than a mile from the campus?".

    a) has

    b) Did they

    c) less than

267. Choose the wrong word: "Some conifers, that is, tree that have cones, are able to thrive on poor, thin soil.".

    a) Some

    b) that is

    c) tree

268. Choose the wrong word: "Consequently the kit fox is an endangered species, wildlife experts are using various methods to protect it.".

    a) Consequently

b) are using

c) an

269. Choose the wrong word: "Fertilizers are used primarily to enrich the soil and increasing yield.".

    a) are used

    b) increasing

    c) the soil

270. Choose the wrong word: "Sarah buyed her computer from a reputable dealer but she later found out she had been cheated.".

    a) reputable

    b) from

    c) buyed

271. Choose the wrong word: "One can only live without water for about ten days because almost 60 percent of their body is water.".

    a) for

    b) their

    c) because

272. Choose the wrong word: "In the last 10 years, Mexican government has reduced the number of its state-owned companies to about half.".

    a) Mexican

    b) has reduced

    c) its

273. Choose the wrong word: "Their silly, whiny conversation on a child level was meant to create tension and heighten Mary's fears and anxiety.".

    a) to create

    b) heighten

    c) on a child level

274. Choose the wrong word: "Not one in one hundred children exposed to the disease are likely to develop symptoms of it.".

    a) likely

    b) are

    c) to develop

275. Choose the wrong word: "There is some scissors in the desk drawer in the bedroom if you need them.".

    a) is

b) scissors

c) in

276. Choose the wrong word: "The freshman failed to follow the advice of her senior that he studied hard and not go out too much.".

    a) freshman

    b) studied

    c) go out

277. Choose the wrong word: "Earwax lubricates and protects the ear from foreign matter such water and insects.".

    a) foreign

    b) insects

    c) such

278. Choose the wrong word: "How the Earth is in the shadow of the moon, we see an eclipse of the sun.".

    a) How

    b) in the shadow

    c) an

279. Choose the wrong word: "The MX is a four-stages rocket with an 8,000-mile range, larger than that of the Minuteman.".

    a) larger than

    b) a four-stages

    c) an 8,000

280. Choose the wrong word: "People from temperate climates cannot survive for long in temperatures extreme.".

    a) from

    b) for long

    c) temperatures extreme

281. Choose the wrong word: "Because of the severe snow storm and the road blocks, the air force dropped food and medical supplies close the city.".

    a) the

    b) dropped food

    c) close the city

282. Choose the wrong word: "As every other nation, the United States used to define its unit of currency, the dollar, in terms of the gold

standard.".

    a) As

    b) other

    c) used to define

283. Choose the wrong word: "A farmer's tractor is like a powerful horse, as it plows field, pulls trailers and moves heavy loads.".

    a) as it

    b) field

    c) moves

284. Choose the wrong word: "Many different combination of foods can give us the essentials we need for an adequate diet.".

    a) combination

    b) foods

    c) an adequate

285. Choose the wrong word: "We are suppose to real all of chapters seven and answer the questions for tomorrow's class.".

    a) all of chapters

    b) answer

    c) suppose to

286. Choose the wrong word: "This party was one of the two major political powers in the country from 1920 and 1935.".

    a) one of

    b) political powers

    c) and 1935

287. Choose the wrong word: "By passing sunlight through a prism, the light is separate into a spectrum of colors.".

    a) is separate

    b) through

    c) spectrum

288. Choose the wrong word: "The scientific method consists of forming hypotheses, collect data and testing results.".

    a) results

    b) collect

    c) scientific

289. Choose the wrong word: "In spite of the inclement weather the tennis tournament went ahead just as the players had started putting their rackets into.".

    a) in spite of

    b) ahead

    c) rackets into

290. Choose the wrong word: "Putting a large amount of information on a map, a variety of symbols are used.".

    a) Putting

    b) variety of

    c) are used

291. Choose the wrong word: "Having lost the election, the presidential candidate intends supporting the opposition despite the objections of his stall.".

    a) despite

    b) supporting

    c) objections of

292. Choose the wrong word: "Because early balloons were at the mercy of shifting winds, they are not considered a practical means of transportation until the 1860s.".

    a) Because

    b) shifting

    c) are

293. Choose the wrong word: "Kiwi birds search the ground with the bills for insects, worms and snails to eat.".

    a) the

    b) insects

    c) search

294. Choose the wrong word: "The diary it was kept secret until the end of the war in fear of reprisals by the occupying army.".

    a) secret

    b) in fear of

    c) it

295. Choose the wrong word: "Since vitamins are contained in a wide variety of foods, people seldom lack of most of them.".

a) lack of

b) in a

c) variety of

296. Choose the wrong word: "The new mall shopping in the downtown area will be more expensive for shoppers than the mall on the freeway outside the town.".

a) the mall

b) shopping

c) downtown

297. Choose the wrong word: "West of the river have vast plains over which the wagon trains labored ignoring them in favor of dreams of gold and richer land further west.".

a) further west

b) have

c) West of

298. Choose the wrong word: "The classification of a dinosaur as either type 1 nor type 2 depends on the structure of the hip.".

a) depends on

b) as

c) nor

299. Choose the wrong word: "Salmon lay their eggs and die in freshwater, although they live in salt water when most of their adult lives.".

a) when

b) although

c) lay

300. Choose the wrong word: "Into among the five Great Lakes, only Lake Michigan is located entirely within the territorial boundaries of the US.".

a) is located

b) Into among

c) entirely

301. Choose the wrong word: "Mark Twain's latest work are one of America's national treasures.".

a) national

b) of

c) are

302. Choose the wrong word: "Almost poetry is more enjoyable when it is read aloud.".

    a) Almost

    b) more enjoyable

    c) it is

303. Choose the wrong word: "Lasers are indispensable tools for delicate eyes surgery.".

    a) tools

    b) eyes

    c) are

304. Choose the wrong word: "Caesar, to please themselves, killed his mother, his brother and all his advisers, and finally killed himself out of self-love.".

    a) himself

    b) themselves

    c) his advisers

305. Choose the wrong word: "Pele scored more as 1,200 goals during his career, gaining a reputation as the best soccer player of all time.".

    a) more as

    b) during his career

    c) gaining

306. Choose the wrong word: "Some bacteria are extremely harmful, but anothers are regularly used in producing cheeses, crackers and many other foods.".

    a) are extremely

    b) anothers

    c) regularly

307. Choose the wrong word: "Quality control studies show that employees work the most efficient when they are involved in the total operation rather than in only one part of it.".

    a) in

    b) involved in

    c) efficient

308. Choose the wrong word: "After the yolk separated from the white, it must be boil immediately.".

a) separated

b) boil

c) from the

309. Choose the wrong word: "The library at the university is new and has taken her name from the wife of the first president of the university.".

a) her

b) has taken

c) of the first

310. Choose the wrong word: "Only rarely wins the same major league baseball team the World Series two years in a row.".

a) in a row

b) two years

c) wins the same major league baseball team

311. Choose the wrong word: "Since lightning was probably significant in the formation of life, understanding it might help us to understanding life itself.".

a) might help

b) itself

c) to understanding

312. Choose the wrong word: "According to the Fifth Amendment to the U.S. Constitution, no person should be compelled to be a witness against him own.".

a) him own

b) should be compelled

c) no

313. Choose the wrong word: "Friendship, stability and trusty are frequently mentioned as criteria for a worthwhile relationship between people.".

a) trusty

b) between

c) mentioned

314. Choose the wrong word: "Despite of the increase in air fares, most people still prefer to travel by plane.".

a) prefer

b) to travel

c) Despite of

315. Choose the wrong word: "Gunpowder, in some ways the most effective of all the explosive materials, were a mixture of potassium nitrate, charcoal and sulfur.".

    a) in some ways

    b) were

    c) all

316. Choose the wrong word: "The children's television program called "The lonely cats" was seeing in 84 countries in 1989.".

    a) called

    b) in

    c) seeing

317. Choose the wrong word: "Today's job seekers are confronted with such question as "Are you computer literate?" and "Can you set up a data base?".".

    a) set up

    b) such question

    c) confronted

318. Choose the wrong word: "A galaxy, where may include billions of stars, is held together by gravitational attraction.".

    a) where

    b) of

    c) by

319. Choose the wrong word: "People with exceptionally high intelligence quotients may not be the best employees since they become bored of their work unless the job is constantly changing.".

    a) changing

    b) the best

    c) bored of

320. Choose the wrong word: "One of history's most spectacular executions were that of Damiens.".

    a) One of

    b) were

    c) most spectacular

321. Choose the wrong word: "Mrs. Smith bought last week a new sports car; however, she has yet to learn how to operate the manual gearshift.".

    a) last week a new sports car

    b) however

    c) has yet to learn

322. Choose the wrong word: "As the numeral of older people increases, services for the elderly will soon represent one of the fastest-growing areas of employment.".

    a) numeral

    b) older people

    c) areas

323. Choose the wrong word: "The disposable camera, a single-use camera preloaded with print film, has appeared in the late 1980s and has become very popular.".

    a) preloaded with

    b) has become

    c) has appeared

324. Choose the wrong word: "When the ball struck him in the face, the player was collapsed but his teammates carried on playing.".

    a) was collapsed

    b) in the face

    c) carried on

325. Choose the wrong word: "Nutritionists recommend that foods from each of the four basic groups be eaten on a regularly daily basis.".

    a) from each of

    b) regularly

    c) recommend

326. Choose the wrong word: "Psychologists at the University of Boston has studied the effects of the color of a room on people's behaviour.".

    a) has studied

    b) effects

    c) color

327. Choose the wrong word: "Each of the Intelsat satellites remain in a fixed position from which they relay radio signals to more than seventy earth stations.".

a) fixed

b) more than

c) remain

328. Choose the wrong word: "Whereas Earth has one moon, the planet call Mars has two small ones.".

a) Whereas

b) call

c) has

329. Choose the wrong word: "The prices of homes are as high in urban areas that most young people cannot afford to buy them.".

a) most

b) as

c) them

330. Choose the wrong word: "She has decided to take a same classes as you next semester hoping you will help her.".

a) a same

b) next

c) hoping

331. Choose the wrong word: "In England as early as the twelfth century, young boys enjoyed to play football.".

a) to play

b) as early as

c) In England

332. Choose the wrong word: "Sarah said that she went to the supermarket before coming home.".

a) before coming

b) went

c) that

333. Choose the wrong word: "Before his death in 1943, in an effort to encourage less dependence on one crop by the South, Washington Carver is responsible for developing hundreds of industrial uses for peanuts and sweet potatoes.".

a) less dependence

b) is

c) uses

334. Choose the wrong word: "To receive a degree from an American university, one must take many courses beside those in one's major field.".

    a) those

    b) To receive

    c) beside

335. Choose the wrong word: "In Ground Control Approach, the air traffic controller informs the pilot how far is the plane from the touchdown point.".

    a) is the plane

    b) informs

    c) the touchdown point

336. Choose the wrong word: "By the turn of the century, most of the inventions that were to bring in all the comforts of modern living have already been thought of.".

    a) that

    b) were to

    c) have already been

337. Choose the wrong word: "Richard Smith, an invention best known for the development of that gun, actually put most of his effort into improving agricultural methods.".

    a) actually

    b) invention

    c) most of

338. Choose the wrong word: "The greater number of dentists in smallest towns shows either that dentists don't like big cities or there are now more dentists.".

    a) big cities

    b) more

    c) smallest

339. Choose the wrong word: "Many birds will, in the normal course of their migrations, flying more than three thousand miles to reach their winter homes.".

    a) flying

    b) to reach

    c) more than three thousand miles

340. Choose the wrong word: "Heartburn can best be understood as a symptom causing by acid reflux due to a weak lower esophageal sphincter.".

    a) best be

    b) weak

    c) causing by

341. Choose the wrong word: "Although Daniel Smith lived only a few months with the artificial heart, doctors were able to learn a great deal from him having used it.".

    a) used

    b) him

    c) a few months

342. Choose the wrong word: "In most states insurance agents must pass an examination to be licensed when they will complete their training.".

    a) will complete

    b) must pass

    c) most states

343. Choose the wrong word: "Drug abuse have become one of America's most serious social problems.".

    a) one of

    b) most

    c) have

344. Choose the wrong word: "Sarah hardly never misses an opportunity to play in the tennis tournaments.".

    a) never

    b) to play

    c) an

345. Choose the wrong word: "After Dr. Smith discovered restriction enzymes, Dr. James, Brian Pawsey and him were awarded the Nobel prize for their research in that field.".

    a) were awarded

    b) him

    c) discovered

346. Choose the wrong word: "During visiting the new footwear plant, the members of the group were introduced to all the latest styles in sports

shoes.".

    a) During

    b) were introduced

    c) sports

347. Choose the wrong word: "Her bilingual ability and previous experience were the qualities that which helped her get the job over all the other candidates.".

    a) were

    b) helped her

    c) that which

348. Choose the wrong word: "Globes and maps have been important throughout history, but never many so than today.".

    a) many

    b) have been important

    c) than

349. Choose the wrong word: "The new librarian was hired because of her past experience has been found to be not only inefficient but also lazy.".

    a) but also

    b) been found

    c) was hired

350. Choose the wrong word: "Water ice, and snow play a role in affecting an earth's rotation.".

    a) Water

    b) an earth's

    c) rotation

351. Choose the wrong word: "Though Picasso was primarily a painting, he also became a fine sculptor, engraver and ceramist.".

    a) fine

    b) painting

    c) primarily

352. Choose the wrong word: "These televisions are quite popular in Europe, but those ones are not.".

    a) are

    b) quite

    c) those ones

353. Choose the wrong word: "Although they were friends, they did not really form a group since her style differed wide from that of the other two.".

    a) wide

    b) from

    c) the other two

354. Choose the wrong word: "It was only after 1820 that a distinctive American literature had begun to appear with writers like Washington and Cooper.".

    a) It was

    b) to appear

    c) had begun

355. Choose the wrong word: "The chemistry instructor explained the experiment in such of a way that it was easily understood.".

    a) was

    b) such of a way

    c) easily understood

356. Choose the wrong word: "Plants absorb water and nutrients and anchoring themselves in the soil with their roots.".

    a) anchoring themselves

    b) the soil

    c) absorb water

357. Choose the wrong word: "Certain pollens are more likely to cause an allergic reaction than another.".

    a) likely

    b) Certain

    c) another

358. Choose the wrong word: "An uncultivated tea plant might grow about 50 feet height.".

    a) about

    b) tea plant

    c) height

359. Choose the wrong word: "Many of the problems associated with aging such as disorientation and irritability may result from to eat an unbalanced diet.".

a) from to eat

b) may result

c) such as

360. Choose the wrong word: "Even on the most careful prepared trip, problems will sometimes develop.".

a) Even

b) trip

c) careful

361. Choose the wrong word: "Listening to music on tape or even on disk is not nearly as good as to go to a live concert.".

a) even

b) to go

c) live

362. Choose the wrong word: "The first postage stamp, issued in 1860, in England it was the Penny Black, which featured a profile of Queen Victoria.".

a) it was

b) featured

c) the

363. Choose the wrong word: "The bridge at Niagara Falls spans the longer unguarded border in the history of the world, symbolizing the peace and goodwill that exists between Canada and the United States.".

a) exists

b) the longer

c) between

364. Choose the wrong word: "Today we know that the Earth is one of nine planets who orbit the sun.".

a) we

b) orbit

c) who

365. Choose the wrong word: "She is looking forward to go Europe after she finished her studies at the university.".

a) to go

b) finishes

c) looking

366. Choose the wrong word: "If you don't register before the last day of regular registration, you paying a late fee.".

    a) the last day

    b) a late fee

    c) paying

367. Choose the wrong word: "The actor failed to show at the rehearsal because his migraine.".

    a) failed

    b) because

    c) show at

368. Choose the wrong word: "An unexpected raise in the cost of living as well as a decline in employment opportunities has resulted in the rapid creation by Congress of new government programs for the unemployed.".

    a) raise

    b) as well as

    c) resulted in

369. Choose the wrong word: "Traditionally, the flag is risen in the morning and taken down at night.".

    a) taken

    b) at night

    c) risen

370. Choose the wrong word: "Acute pharyngitis pain is most often caused by a viral infection, for who antibiotics are ineffective.".

    a) caused by

    b) are ineffective

    c) who

371. Choose the wrong word: "Neither of the two candidates who had applied for admission to the IED were eligible for admission.".

    a) who

    b) were

    c) had applied

372. Choose the wrong word: "As the Asian economic miracle spreads throughout the Pacific, wage increases everywhere is affecting millions of consumers.".

    a) is

b) spreads

c) As

373. Choose the wrong word: "Many architects prefer that a dome is used to roof buildings that need to conserve floor space.".

    a) to conserve

    b) floor space

    c) is used

374. Choose the wrong word: "Increasing involvement in agriculture by large corporations has resulted in what is knows as agribusiness, that is, agriculture with business techniques and to control all stages of the operations.".

    a) by large corporations

    b) to control

    c) known as

375. Choose the wrong word: "Studying the science of logic is one way to cultivate one's reason skills.".

    a) way to

    b) science of

    c) reason

376. Choose the wrong word: "Species like snakes, lizards, coyotes, squirrels and jack rabbits seems to exist quite happily in the desert.".

    a) seems to

    b) like

    c) quite happily

377. Choose the wrong word: "Many states do laws regulating production processes for different types of food products.".

    a) regulating

    b) types of

    c) do

378. Choose the wrong word: "President Wilson had hoped that World War I be the last great war, but only two decades later, the Second World War was erupting.".

    a) was erupting

    b) be

    c) later

379. Choose the wrong word: "According to legend, because the Indian Princess Pocahontas said that she loved he, Captain Smith was set free.".

    a) he

    b) because

    c) According to

380. Choose the wrong word: "The value of precious gems is determined by their hardness, color and brilliant.".

    a) gems

    b) their

    c) brilliant

381. Choose the wrong word: "A lunch of soup and sandwiches do not appeal to all of the students.".

    a) appeal to all of

    b) of

    c) do

382. Choose the wrong word: "Anyone reproducing copyrighted works without permission of the holders of the copyright are breaking the law.".

    a) breaking

    b) are

    c) reproducing

383. Choose the wrong word: "The amount of books in the Library of Congress is more than 5 million volumes.".

    a) The amount

    b) more than

    c) in the Library of Congress

384. Choose the wrong word: "Before the invention of the musical staff, people passed musical compositions on to each other not by writing them down but also by remembering them.".

    a) Before

    b) each other

    c) but also

385. Choose the wrong word: "Before bridges were built, the transport across major rivers in the US were by ferryboat.".

    a) bridges

b) were

c) by

386. Choose the wrong word: "Diamonds are evaluated on the basis of their weigh, purity and color.".

    a) their

    b) are evaluated

    c) weigh

387. Choose the wrong word: "The members of both the House of Representatives and the Senate are election by the citizens of the United States.".

    a) election

    b) both

    c) citizens

388. Choose the wrong word: "The geology professor showed us a sample about volcanic rock which dated back seven hundred years.".

    a) back

    b) about

    c) The

389. Choose the wrong word: "It was her who represented her country in the United Nations and later became ambassador to the United States.".

    a) who

    b) later

    c) her

390. Choose the wrong word: "When two products are basically the same as, advertising can influence the public's choice.".

    a) the same as

    b) basically

    c) influence

391. Choose the wrong word: "If protect, a solar cell lasts for a long time and is a good source of energy.".

    a) protect

    b) solar

    c) source of

392. Choose the wrong word: "The committee decided to have biannual meetings together with families to be held every six months at the

64

beach.".

    a) to have

    b) with

    c) every six moths

393. Choose the wrong word: "As you come to each town, however small, you will see a sign which states the name of the town and how many inhabitants does it have.".

    a) however small

    b) will

    c) does it have

394. Choose the wrong word: "The Impressionists like Monet and Manet known to use color in order to create an image of reality rather than reality itself.".

    a) to create

    b) known

    c) like

395. Choose the wrong word: "Despite their insistence that he will appear when there is an important event, the president schedules press conferences with the news media at his discretion.".

    a) there is

    b) will appear

    c) Despite

396. Choose the wrong word: "Nobel prizes are awarded to people who excellent in their fields above and beyond what is expected from scholars.".

    a) who excellent

    b) are awarded

    c) and beyond

397. Choose the wrong word: "Mr. Burbank was a pioneer in the process of graft immature plants onto fully mature plants.".

    a) a pioneer

    b) fully

    c) graft

398. Choose the wrong word: "I do not know where could he have gone so early in the morning.".

a) gone

b) so early

c) could he have

399. Choose the wrong word: "Disease is not as widespread than before because of better preventive medicine and vastly improved nutrition.".

a) Disease

b) than before

c) better

400. Choose the wrong word: "The Secret Garden, it is a book written years ago for children, has become popular again among adults in the film version.".

a) it is a book

b) years ago

c) film version

401. Choose the wrong word: "The National Park, where is there oddly shaped and magnificently colored rock formations, is located in southern Utah.".

a) formations

b) is there

c) oddly shaped

402. Choose the wrong word: "I had received my book back from Brian; I could have lent it to you.".

a) back from

b) lent

c) I had

403. Choose the wrong word: "The bodies of cold-blooded animals have the same temperature their surroundings, but those of warm-blooded animals do not.".

a) the same temperature

b) do not

c) have

404. Choose the wrong word: "Because of differences between the crops gown and a greater abundance of rivers, farmers in the South need little rain than their counterparts in the North.".

a) farmers

b) differences between

c) little

405. Choose the wrong word: "Mined over 1,500 years ago, copper is one of the earliest know metals.".

    a) Mined

    b) ago

    c) know

406. Choose the wrong word: "Mercury is not often visible because it is so near the sun to be seen.".

    a) so

    b) near the sun

    c) Mercury

407. Choose the wrong word: "His story is a clinical portrayal of man as an animal trapped by the fear and hunger.".

    a) of man as an animal

    b) the fear and hunger

    c) His

408. Choose the wrong word: "The new technique calls for heat the mixture before applying it to the wood.".

    a) applying

    b) heat

    c) calls

409. Choose the wrong word: "Although blood lets a residue in urine and stool samples, it cannot always be detected without the aid of a microscope.".

    a) lets

    b) be detected

    c) blood

410. Choose the wrong word: "Students in the United States often support themselves by babysitting, working in restaurants or they drive taxicabs.".

    a) often

    b) themselves

    c) they drive

411. Choose the wrong word: "After writing it the essay must be duplicated by the student himself and handed into the department

secretary before the end of the month.".
- a) After writing it
- b) into
- c) the end of

412. Choose the wrong word: "Gold, silver and copper coins are often alloyed with harder metals to make them hard as enough to withstand wear.".
- a) them
- b) to make
- c) hard as enough

413. Choose the wrong word: "Because his efforts and those of the people who worked with him, human beings no longer fear the dreaded disease of yellow fever.".
- a) no longer
- b) Because
- c) dreaded disease

414. Choose the wrong word: "Some fish use their sense of smell as a guide when return to a spawning site.".
- a) return
- b) fish
- c) as

415. Choose the wrong word: "Antique auctions are getting more and more popular in the United States because increasing public awareness of the value of investing in antiques.".
- a) more and more
- b) auctions
- c) because

416. Choose the wrong word: "The cacao bean was cultivated by the Aztecs not only to drink but also currency.".
- a) was cultivated
- b) but also
- c) currency

417. Choose the wrong word: "Her application for a visa was turned down not only because it was incomplete and incorrectly filled out but also because it was written in pencil.".

a) incomplete

b) for a visa

c) down

418. Choose the wrong word: "Before she moved here, Arlene had been president of the organization since four years.".

    a) Before

    b) since

    c) been

419. Choose the wrong word: "They are going to have to leave soon and so do we.".

    a) leave soon

    b) to have to

    c) so do

420. Choose the wrong word: "Steve lived in New York since 1960 to 1975, but he is now living in Boston.".

    a) since

    b) is now living

    c) in

421. Choose the wrong word: "The continental shelves is the shallow area of the ocean floor that is closest to the continents.".

    a) ocean floor

    b) shelves

    c) closest to

422. Choose the wrong word: "I certainly appreciate him telling us about the delay in delivering the materials because we had planned to begin work tomorrow.".

    a) telling

    b) delivering

    c) him

423. Choose the wrong word: "The pilot and the crew divided the life preservers between the twenty frantic passengers.".

    a) between

    b) divided

    c) and the crew

424. Choose the wrong word: "The information officer at the bank told his customers that there was several different kinds of checking accounts available.".

    a) at the bank

    b) there was

    c) told

425. Choose the wrong word: "The higher the solar activity, the intense the auroras or polar light displays in the skies near the earth's geomagnetic poles.".

    a) near

    b) the auroras

    c) the intense

426. Choose the wrong word: "In order to receive full reimbursement for jewelry that might be stolen, the owner must get all pieces appraise.".

    a) appraise

    b) be stolen

    c) to receive

427. Choose the wrong word: "On the fourth July in 1884, the Statue of Liberty was presented formally by the people of France to the people of the United States.".

    a) presented

    b) the fourth July

    c) formally

428. Choose the wrong word: "Sarah giving up smoking has caused him to gain weight and become irritable with his acquaintances.".

    a) Sarah

    b) smoking has

    c) become irritable

429. Choose the wrong word: "The twinkling lights of the firefly are signals so that the male and female of the species can find each to the other.".

    a) so that

    b) are

    c) each to the other

430. Choose the wrong word: "Malnutrition is a major cause of death in those countries where the cultivation of rice have been impeded by

recurrent drought.".

    a) is a major

    b) have

    c) in those countries

431. Choose the wrong word: "In the 1800's botanist Anne Gray worked to describe and classifying the plants found in North America.".

    a) classifying

    b) botanist

    c) worked

432. Choose the wrong word: "Graphology the science of handwriting analysis, has interested people as far back as the 2nd century.".

    a) as far back as

    b) the science

    c) has interested

433. Choose the wrong word: "Most presidential candidates have their names print on the ballot in this state primary election because it is customarily the first one in the nation, and winning it can give them a good chance to be nominated by their parties.".

    a) print

    b) the first one

    c) it is

434. Choose the wrong word: "Cartilage covers the ends of bones helps to protect the joints from wear and tear.".

    a) the end

    b) covers

    c) to protect

435. Choose the wrong word: "If drivers obeyed the speed limit, fewer accidents occur.".

    a) drivers

    b) fewer

    c) occur

436. Choose the wrong word: "It is interesting to compare the early stylized art forms of ancient civilizations to the modern abstract forms of art.".

    a) interesting

b) to

c) of

437. Choose the wrong word: "He not only composed popular songs for musicals, also wrote more serious concerts.".

    a) composed

    b) more serious

    c) also

438. Choose the wrong word: "Pioneers on the plains sometimes living in dugouts, sod rooms cut into hillsides.".

    a) living

    b) on the

    c) cut into

439. Choose the wrong word: "The average salt content of seawater is more than three percents.".

    a) more than

    b) percents

    c) content

440. Choose the wrong word: "The progress made in space travel for the early 1960s is remarkable.".

    a) progress

    b) made

    c) for

441. Choose the wrong word: "To estimate how much it will cost to build a home, finding the total square footage of the house and multiply by cost per square foot.".

    a) finding

    b) it will cost

    c) by cost

442. Choose the wrong word: "In 1960 it was naively predicted that eight or ten computer would be sufficient to handle all of the scientific and business needs in the United States.".

    a) naively

    b) to handle

    c) eight or ten computer

443. Choose the wrong word: "The examination will test your ability to understand spoken English, to read non-technical language, and writing correctly.".

    a) spoken

    b) writing

    c) will test

444. Choose the wrong word: "The first living structures to appear on earth thousands of years ago were alike viruses.".

    a) alike

    b) to appear

    c) ago

445. Choose the wrong word: "Often when the weather is extremely hot, people have very thirsty but are not terribly hungry.".

    a) Often

    b) but

    c) have

446. Choose the wrong word: "The coal is the world's most abundant fossil fuel.".

    a) The coal

    b) fossil

    c) fuel

447. Choose the wrong word: "In 1784 Benjamin Franklin first suggested daylight savings time as a means of cutting down on consumes candles.".

    a) cutting

    b) consumes candles

    c) means

448. Choose the wrong word: "All the students are looking forward spending their free time relaxing in the sun this summer.".

    a) students

    b) are

    c) forward spending

449. Choose the wrong word: "The company representative sold to the manager a sewing machine for forty dollars.".

    a) to the manager

b) sewing

c) for

450. Choose the wrong word: "No other quality is more important for a scientist to acquire as to observe carefully.".

    a) for

    b) as

    c) carefully

451. Choose the wrong word: "There are twenty species of wild roses in North America, all of which have prickly stems, pinnate leaves and large flowers, which usually smell sweetly.".

    a) sweetly

    b) which

    c) have

452. Choose the wrong word: "Many people don't know that horses can in fact to swim better than many other animals.".

    a) that

    b) to swim

    c) many other

453. Choose the wrong word: "The growth rate of the Pacific Rim countries is five times fast as comparable areas during the Industrial Revolution.".

    a) growth rate

    b) during

    c) times

454. Choose the wrong word: "It has been suggestioned that the battleship be brought back to active duty, at a cost of nearly $500 million.".

    a) suggestioned

    b) has been

    c) active

455. Choose the wrong word: "Energy in a tornado is enormous by any set of standards.".

    a) a tornado

    b) Energy

    c) standards

456. Choose the wrong word: "While verbalization is the most common form of language in existence, humans make use of many others systems and techniques to express their thoughts and feelings.".

    a) others systems

    b) existence

    c) to express

457. Choose the wrong word: "Smoking is the number one prevent cause of death in the United States.".

    a) Smoking

    b) of death

    c) prevent

458. Choose the wrong word: "If you will buy one box at the regular price, you would receive another one at no extra cost.".

    a) no

    b) another one

    c) will buy

459. Choose the wrong word: "The equipment in the office was badly in need of to be repaired.".

    a) equipment

    b) to be repaired

    c) was badly

460. Choose the wrong word: "The governor has not decided how to deal with the new problems already.".

    a) has

    b) how to deal

    c) already

461. Choose the wrong word: "It is the troposphere, the lowest part of the atmosphere, that wind, stormy and other kinds of weather take place.".

    a) the lowest part

    b) take place

    c) stormy

462. Choose the wrong word: "Insulin, it is used to treat diabetes and is secured chiefly from the pancreas of cattle and hogs.".

    a) to treat

b) it is

c) chiefly from

463. Choose the wrong word: "The people tried of defending their village, but they were finally forced to retreat.".

    a) of defending

    b) forced

    c) their

464. Choose the wrong word: "When rhinos take mud baths, the mud create a barrier to biting insects.".

    a) biting

    b) create

    c) When

465. Choose the wrong word: "When Columbus seen the New World, he thought that he had reached the East Indies by way of a Western route.".

    a) had reached

    b) by way of

    c) seen

466. Choose the wrong word: "According to the theory of natural selection, the man who was able to use the hands and feet most freely to walk and grasp was the one who survived and evolved.".

    a) the hands and feet

    b) freely

    c) who

467. Choose the wrong word: "It is said that the American flag has five-pointed stars because Betsy Ross told General Washington she would rather that he changing the six-pointed ones.".

    a) she

    b) changing

    c) It is said

468. Choose the wrong word: "The family decided to call the doctor, who very soon after the call, because the old lady took a turn for the worse.".

    a) very soon

    b) the call

    c) the worse

469. Choose the wrong word: "The railroad was one of the first methods of transportation to be use extensively in early American history.".

    a) one

    b) the first

    c) use

470. Choose the wrong word: "The famous aviator Lindbergh was a early supporter of rocket research.".

    a) famous aviator

    b) supporter

    c) a

471. Choose the wrong word: "A neutrino is a subatomic particle it has no electrical charge.".

    a) a subatomic

    b) no

    c) it

472. Choose the wrong word: "Fireflies product light through a complex chemical reaction that takes place within their abdominal cells.".

    a) product

    b) complex

    c) that takes

473. Choose the wrong word: "Hummingbirds move their wings so rapid a way that they appear to be hanging in the air.".

    a) in the air

    b) rapid a way

    c) their

474. Choose the wrong word: "An octopus has three heart to pump blood throughout their body.".

    a) their

    b) pump blood

    c) throughout

475. Choose the wrong word: "A new form of cocaine, crack attacks the nervous system, brain and bodily in a sharper fashion than cocaine.".

    a) form

    b) bodily

    c) attacks

476. Choose the wrong word: "Most fungi are scavengers who grow on the remains of plants and animals, causing them to decay and change into rich soil.".

    a) are scavengers

    b) the remains

    c) who grow

477. Choose the wrong word: "The ATM cards the principal means for getting cash quickly is in most countries.".

    a) is

    b) quickly

    c) the principal

478. Choose the wrong word: "The National Research Center which was established in 1982 by Mrs. Johnson on sixty acres of land east of the city.".

    a) which was

    b) east of

    c) on sixty acres

479. Choose the wrong word: "Crocodiles different from alligators in that they have pointed snouts and long lower teeth that stick out when their mouths are closed.".

    a) are closed

    b) different from

    c) pointed snouts

480. Choose the wrong word: "Venomous snakes with modified teeth connected to poison glands in which the venom is secreted and stored.".

    a) in which

    b) poison glands

    c) with

481. Choose the wrong word: "Scientists had previously estimated that the Grand Canyon is ten million years old; but now, by using a more modern dating method, they agree that the age is closer to six million years.".

    a) is

    b) by using

    c) previously

482. Choose the wrong word: "Statistics show that the greatest number of B.A. degrees in recent years has been conferring in the fields of business management, education and social sciences.".

    a) show

    b) the

    c) has been conferring

483. Choose the wrong word: "Many heavy work that was one done by hand can now be done more easily with the help of compressed air.".

    a) Many

    b) done

    c) by hand

484. Choose the wrong word: "With its compound eyes, dragonflies can see moving insects approximately 18 feet away.".

    a) moving

    b) its

    c) feet

485. Choose the wrong word: "One and more sentences related to the same topic form a paragraph.".

    a) related to

    b) form

    c) and

486. Choose the wrong word: "The electrical activity of the brain causes the transmission of brain waves that can be recorded and interpreted in terms that explains the types of mental activity.".

    a) that

    b) explains

    c) interpreted

487. Choose the wrong word: "Bahama Islands comprising over 100 islands, are situated just off the southwestern coast of Florida.".

    a) Bahama Islands

    b) over

    c) comprising

488. Choose the wrong word: "The lab assistants has to take over from the students who monitoring the experiment because they became tired.".

    a) has to

b) who monitoring

c) they

489. Choose the wrong word: "The president refuses to accept either of the four new proposals made by the contractors.".

    a) to accept

    b) either

    c) made by

490. Choose the wrong word: "The most popular breed of dog in the United States are cocker spaniel, poddle and retriever.".

    a) breed

    b) The most

    c) in the

491. Choose the wrong word: "The United States is the world's largest cheese producer making more than two million tons of cheese annual.".

    a) world's

    b) making

    c) annual

492. Choose the wrong word: "When Cliff was sick with the flu, his mother made him to eat chicken soup and rest in bed.".

    a) to eat

    b) him

    c) rest

493. Choose the wrong word: "Although the Indians and the Eskimo had lived for centuries in Canada and the United States, when the settlers came in the seventeenth century, the newcomers began a systematic effort to push their into the wilderness.".

    a) to push

    b) their

    c) in the seventeenth

494. Choose the wrong word: "In present-day business entrepreneurs are taken fewer risks then their predecessors a century ago.".

    a) present-day

    b) fewer

    c) are taken

495. Choose the wrong word: "Many American childrens learned to read using these books.".

      a) to read

      b) childrens

      c) using

496. Choose the wrong word: "Almost the plants known to us are made up of a great many cells, specialized to perform different tasks.".

      a) a great many cells

      b) to perform

      c) Almost

497. Choose the wrong word: "Because the interstate highway system linking roads across the country was built about thirty-five years ago, most of the roads in the system now need repaired.".

      a) repaired

      b) was built

      c) Because

498. Choose the wrong word: "Some methods to prevent soil erosion are plowing parallel with the slopes of hills, to plant trees on unproductive land and rotating crops.".

      a) Some

      b) to prevent

      c) to plant

499. Choose the wrong word: "I put my new book of zoology here on the desk a few minutes ago, but I cannot seem to find it.".

      a) the desk

      b) book of zoology

      c) ago

500. Choose the wrong word: "What he was much better than me at chess became apparent after the first few minutes of the game.".

      a) What

      b) became

      c) first few

Set II

501. Choose the wrong word: "Sarah said she would borrow me her new movie camera if I wanted to use it on my trip to Europe.".

    a) borrow

    b) I wanted

    c) on my trip

502. Choose the wrong word: "If the project if finished on time, the federal government won't award the company further contracts.".

    a) award

    b) further

    c) If

503. Choose the wrong word: "That it is the moon influences only one kind of tide is not generally known.".

    a) one kind

    b) it is

    c) generally

504. Choose the wrong word: "Rock music was original a mixture of country music and rhythm and blues.".

    a) Rock music

    b) original

    c) country music

505. Choose the wrong word: "Accurate meteorological predictions can be formulated using techniques derived from chemicals, physics and mathematics.".

    a) derived

    b) predictions

    c) chemicals

506. Choose the wrong word: "The Zoning Improvement Plan, better known as zip codes, enable postal clerks to speed the routing of an ever-increasing volume of mail.".

    a) enable

    b) to speed

    c) an

507. Choose the wrong word: "Before dinosaurs became extinct, plant life is very different on Earth.".

    a) became

    b) is

    c) different

508. Choose the wrong word: "The Columbine flower can survive in almost any type of gardens condition in the United States.".

    a) can

    b) in

    c) gardens

509. Choose the wrong word: "Mrs. Adams had already established Hull House in Chicago and began her work in the Women's Suffrage Movement when she was awarded the Nobel prize.".

    a) began

    b) already

    c) in Chicago

510. Choose the wrong word: "During Jackson's administration, those who did not approve of permit common people in the White House were shocked by the president's insistence that they be invited into the mansion.".

    a) who

    b) permit

    c) be invited

511. Choose the wrong word: "The president, with his wife and daughter, are returning from a brief vacation at Sun Valley in order to attend a press conference this afternoon.".

    a) from

    b) to attend

    c) are

512. Choose the wrong word: "Fertilize farmland is one of the biggest natural resources in the Central States.".

    a) Fertilize

    b) one

    c) biggest

513. Choose the wrong word: "The Cabinet consists of secretaries of departments, who report to the president, give him advice and helping him make decisions.".

    a) consists of

    b) helping

    c) make

514. Choose the wrong word: "Ever the Senate passes a bill, a messenger takes it to the House of Representatives, delivers it to the Speaker of the House, and bows deeply from the waist.".

    a) passes

    b) deeply

    c) Ever

515. Choose the wrong word: "We thought he is planning to go on vacation after the first of the month.".

    a) is

    b) after

    c) the first

516. Choose the wrong word: "Most newspapers depend on the wire services from their international stories and photographs.".

    a) Most

    b) from

    c) on

517. Choose the wrong word: "Having been beaten by the police for striking an officer, the man will cry out in pain.".

    a) by

    b) will cry out

    c) the man

518. Choose the wrong word: "The most common form of treatment it is mass inoculation and chlorination of water sources.".

    a) it

    b) The most common

    c) of

519. Choose the wrong word: "They asked me what did happen last night, but I was unable to tell them.".

    a) unable to

b) tell them

c) what did happen

520. Choose the wrong word: "In 1920s Lindbergh was the first to fly solo nonstop from New York to Paris in such short time.".

    a) was

    b) such short time

    c) to fly

521. Choose the wrong word: "I don't care you do just so long as you do it immediately.".

    a) don't care

    b) do

    c) you do

522. Choose the wrong word: "The deadbolt is the best lock for entry doors because it is not only inexpensive but installation is easy.".

    a) the best

    b) because

    c) installation is easy

523. Choose the wrong word: "Penicillium is one of the many molds that procedures the antibiotics used to control diseases.".

    a) used

    b) procedures

    c) to control

524. Choose the wrong word: "An able flier, a crow may travel thirty or forty miles the day before it returns home.".

    a) the day

    b) flier

    c) may travel

525. Choose the wrong word: "After talks in Prague yesterday, the Secretary of State returning to Washington.".

    a) talks

    b) After

    c) returning

526. Choose the wrong word: "Before the invention of the printing press, books have been all printed by hand.".

    a) Before

b) the printing

c) have been

527. Choose the wrong word: "Drug addiction has resulted of many destroyed careers and expulsions from school or college.".

    a) expulsions

    b) of

    c) destroyed

528. Choose the wrong word: "Lava, rock fragments and gaseous may all erupt from a volcano.".

    a) rock

    b) erupt

    c) gaseous

529. Choose the wrong word: "Nowhere he could find a good place to study, so he returned to his dorm.".

    a) he could

    b) returned

    c) to study

530. Choose the wrong word: "Public health experts say that the money one spends avoiding illness is less than the cost to be sick.".

    a) avoiding

    b) to be

    c) less

531. Choose the wrong word: "The International Red Cross, which has helped so many nations, won the Nobel Peace Prize three times for their efforts to reduce human suffering.".

    a) their efforts

    b) which

    c) human suffering

532. Choose the wrong word: "Sharks differ from other fish in that their skeletons are made of cartilage instead bone.".

    a) are made

    b) differ from

    c) instead

533. Choose the wrong word: "Most of the magnesium used in the United States comes from the sea water.".

a) Most of

b) the

c) the United States

534. Choose the wrong word: "The medical problems of parents and their children tend to be very similar to because of the hereditary natura of many diseases.".

a) because of

b) to be

c) similar to

535. Choose the wrong word: "The novels of Vonnegut present a desperately comic aware of human nature.".

a) aware

b) present

c) desperately

536. Choose the wrong word: "It was her, Elizabeth I, not her father, King Henry, who led England into the Age of Empire.".

a) who

b) led

c) her

537. Choose the wrong word: "The function of pain is to warn the individual of danger so he can take action to avoid more serious damage.".

a) so

b) to warn

c) serious

538. Choose the wrong word: "The winter storm that raced through the area for the last two day moved east today.".

a) the last

b) that raced

c) day

539. Choose the wrong word: "Perhaps was his own lack of proper schooling that led Horace Mann to struggle for the important reforms in education.".

a) led

b) Perhaps was

c) education

540. Choose the wrong word: "This bridge spans the Hudson River to link New York City also New Jersey.".
    a) also
    b) spans
    c) the

541. Choose the wrong word: "Every scientist knows that gravity is the force that maintains the earth and the planets in its orbits around the sun.".
    a) knows
    b) maintains
    c) its

542. Choose the wrong word: "The plants that they belong to the family of ferns are quite varied in their size and structure.".
    a) belong
    b) they
    c) are

543. Choose the wrong word: "As the marathon runner reached the half-way mark he being hot and was soaked with perspiration stopped to rub himself down with a towel.".
    a) was soaked
    b) marathon
    c) with

544. Choose the wrong word: "Columbus Day is celebrated on the twelve of October because on that day in 1492, Columbus landed in the America.".
    a) is celebrated
    b) twelve
    c) because

545. Choose the wrong word: "The harder he tried, the worst he danced before the large audience.".
    a) large
    b) tried
    c) worst

546. Choose the wrong word: "Although a number of police officers was guarding the priceless treasures in the museum, the director worried that

someone would try to steal them.".

    a) would try

    b) was guarding

    c) to steal

547. Choose the wrong word: "The use of the Computer in Medicine is a new course for senior medical students who if they study and pass will get a special diploma.".

    a) pass

    b) who if

    c) for

548. Choose the wrong word: "Since it was so difficult for American Indians to negotiate a peace treaty or declare war in their native language, they used a universal understood form of sign language.".

    a) universal

    b) so difficult

    c) in their native language

549. Choose the wrong word: "When they have been frightened, as, for example, by an electrical storm, dairy cows may refuse giving milk.".

    a) have been

    b) by

    c) giving

550. Choose the wrong word: "Oceans of the world exerts strong influences on the weather over the Earth's surface.".

    a) on

    b) exerts

    c) surface

551. Choose the wrong word: "In order to survive, trees rely to the amount of annual rainfall they receive, as well as the seasonal distribution of the rain.".

    a) of

    b) as well

    c) rely to

552. Choose the wrong word: "He promised he come on time but he forgot about the heavy traffic at that time of the morning.".

    a) he come

b) on

c) at that time

553. Choose the wrong word: "Wood is still extensively used in construction even though the deterioration causing by weathering is one factor against its use.".

    a) causing

    b) in construction

    c) even

554. Choose the wrong word: "An increasing number of office works use computer programs as daily routine.".

    a) daily

    b) works

    c) of

555. Choose the wrong word: "A water molecule consists of two hydrogen atoms and had one oxygen atom.".

    a) had

    b) A water

    c) atoms

556. Choose the wrong word: "Parks which are found in downtown areas where office workers and store employees can enjoy their lunch hours sitting on the green grass in clean, fresh air.".

    a) which

    b) employees

    c) fresh air

557. Choose the wrong word: "In 1955 the Hawaii was admitted to the Union as the 50th state".

    a) state

    b) the Hawaii

    c) the 50th

558. Choose the wrong word: "The girl whom my cousin married was used to be a chorus girl for the band in Radio City Music Hall in New York.".

    a) was used

    b) whom

    c) The

559. Choose the wrong word: "Some earthworms grow to a very large size, five or six feet in length, but most of them are a little inches long.".

    a) little

    b) some

    c) a

560. Choose the wrong word: "There is about 600 schools in this country that use the Montessori method to encourage individual initiative.".

    a) to encourage

    b) There is

    c) country

561. Choose the wrong word: "Both bowling and ice-skating was introduced by the Dutch who colonized the New World in the 1600s.".

    a) Both

    b) was introduced

    c) colonized

562. Choose the wrong word: "The new shopping mall being painted a bright pink, so potential customers who might otherwise drive past cannot fail to notice it.".

    a) might

    b) fail to

    c) being painted

563. Choose the wrong word: "The isotopes of one element can have different weighs.".

    a) weighs

    b) different

    c) isotopes

564. Choose the wrong word: "The government raises money to operate by tax cigarettes, liquor, gasoline, tires and telephone calls.".

    a) raises

    b) to operate

    c) tax

565. Choose the wrong word: "Oil whale lamps were replaced by kerosene lamps in 1860s and the multi-million dollars whale industry came to an end.".

    a) Oil whale

b) multi-million

c) came

566. Choose the wrong word: "With his father's guidance, Mozart begun playing the clavier at the age of three and composing at the age of five.".

    a) playing

    b) begun

    c) composing

567. Choose the wrong word: "It took eight years to complete the Erie Canal, the 365-mile waterway which it connects Albany and Buffalo in New York State.".

    a) to complete

    b) the 365-mile

    c) which it connects

568. Choose the wrong word: "Have designed his own plane, Mr. Lindbergh flew from Roosevelt Field in New York across the ocean to Le Bourget Field outside Paris.".

    a) flew

    b) outside Paris

    c) Have designed

569. Choose the wrong word: "The hot dog's popularity begun in a small city when a sausage peddler named Feuchtwanger slipped one of his franks into a bun.".

    a) popularity begun

    b) named

    c) slipped

570. Choose the wrong word: "With its strong claws and its many protruding tooth a gopher is an excellent digger.".

    a) strong claws

    b) protruding tooth

    c) With

571. Choose the wrong word: "The taxi driver told the man to don't allow his disobedient son to hang out the window.".

    a) to hang out

    b) taxi driver

    c) to don't allow

572. Choose the wrong word: "Because of his physical, Ben was able to lift the car out of the way.".
> a) physical
> b) able to
> c) Because of

573. Choose the wrong word: "Daniel is particularly fond of cooking, and he often cooks really delicious meals.".
> a) often cooks
> b) really
> c) fond of

574. Choose the wrong word: "The book that you see laying on the table belongs to the teacher.".
> a) that
> b) belongs to
> c) laying

575. Choose the wrong word: "Some tree frogs can alter their colors in order to blend to their environment.".
> a) to
> b) can alter
> c) tree

576. Choose the wrong word: "This novel written after Mrs. Mitchell quit her job as a reporter because of an ankle injury.".
> a) quit
> b) written
> c) as

577. Choose the wrong word: "Those of you who signed up for Dr. Daniel's anthropology class should get their books as soon as possible.".
> a) Those of
> b) as possible
> c) their

578. Choose the wrong word: "A jellyfish, which isn't really a fish, it has no brain, no bones and no face.".
> a) isn't
> b) bones
> c) it

579. Choose the wrong word: "Cotton used to rank first between Alabama's crops, but it represents only a fraction of the agricultural production now.".

   a) rank
   b) between
   c) Cotton

580. Choose the wrong word: "In ancient times and throughout the Middle Ages, many people believed that the earth is motionless.".

   a) is
   b) many people
   c) believed

581. Choose the wrong word: "The change from day to night results the rotation of the Earth.".

   a) the Earth
   b) results
   c) change

582. Choose the wrong word: "Both Yellowstone Park and Wairakei are geothermal areas famous for its hot-spring systems.".

   a) its
   b) hot-spring
   c) are geothermal areas

583. Choose the wrong word: "If a live sponge is broken into pieces, each piece would turn into a new sponge like the original one.".

   a) broken
   b) the original one
   c) would turn

584. Choose the wrong word: "If we were to consider all of the different kinds of motion in discussing the movement of an object, it is very confusing, because even an object at rest is moving as the earth turns.".

   a) different kinds
   b) is
   c) very

585. Choose the wrong word: "The woman at that desk over there will giving you all the information you need to fill out the form.".

   a) The

b) giving

c) out

586. Choose the wrong word: "Having chose the topics for their essays, the students were instructed to make either a preliminary outline or a rough draft.".

    a) Having chose

    b) their

    c) were

587. Choose the wrong word: "Many grasshoppers can produce sounds by rub their hind legs against their wings.".

    a) Many

    b) produce

    c) rub

588. Choose the wrong word: "A calorie is the quantity of heat required to rise one gallon of water one degree centigrade at one atmospheric pressure.".

    a) to rise

    b) required

    c) A calorie

589. Choose the wrong word: "American baseball teams, once the only contenders for the world championship, are now being challenged by either Chinese teams and Japanese teams.".

    a) once

    b) either

    c) being

590. Choose the wrong word: "From 1925 to 1935 the capital of the U.S. will be located in New York City.".

    a) capital

    b) will be

    c) located

591. Choose the wrong word: "This table is not sturdy enough to support a television, and that one probably isn't neither.".

    a) to support

    b) that one

    c) neither

592. Choose the wrong word: "Sheep must have mate in fall since the young are born in early spring every year.".
    a) must have mate
    b) since
    c) are born

593. Choose the wrong word: "The scholarship board selected Daniel because of his research into the effects of vitamins, many of which can be seen in international journals.".
    a) effects
    b) many
    c) international journals

594. Choose the wrong word: "Nobody had known before the presentation that Sarah and her sister will receive the awards for outstanding scholarship.".
    a) had known
    b) the
    c) will receive

595. Choose the wrong word: "In a federal form of government like that of the United States, power is divided between the legislative, executive and judicial branches.".
    a) between
    b) is divided
    c) like

596. Choose the wrong word: "Death Valley is more than 130 kilometers length and no more than 14 kilometers wide.".
    a) no more
    b) length
    c) than

597. Choose the wrong word: "The average adult get two to five colds each year.".
    a) The
    b) to
    c) get

598. Choose the wrong word: "Alike other forms of energy, natural gas may be used to heat homes, cook food and even run automobiles.".

a) Alike

b) to heat

c) may be used

599. Choose the wrong word: "Residents in some cities can call an electrical inspector to have the wiring in their house is checked.".

a) cities

b) is checked

c) an

600. Choose the wrong word: "The Chinese were first and large ethnic group to work on the construction of the transcontinental railroad system.".

a) to work

b) of

c) and large

601. Choose the wrong word: "In the stock market, the fluctuations in Standard and Poor's 500 Index does not always conform to Dow Jones Averages.".

a) does

b) always

c) to

602. Choose the wrong word: "Mary Jones was a prominent figure in the labor movement at the turning of the century.".

a) known

b) a prominent

c) turning

603. Choose the wrong word: "Everyone does not know that words like chicory, cumin, crocus and saffron all come to we from the Sumericans.".

a) does

b) to we

c) all come

604. Choose the wrong word: "The Bill of Right was added to the Constitution specifically to guarantee certain the individual rights.".

a) was added

b) the

c) rights

605. Choose the wrong word: "It is believed that by 1990 immunotherapy have succeeded in curing a number of serious illnesses.".

    a) have succeeded

    b) by 1990

    c) curing

606. Choose the wrong word: "The Nobel prize winning candidate, accompanied by his wife and children, are staying in Sweden until after the presentation.".

    a) by

    b) until

    c) are

607. Choose the wrong word: "Dave's wisdom teeth were troubling him, so he went to a dental surgeon to see about having them pull.".

    a) pull

    b) them

    c) were troubling

608. Choose the wrong word: "Many of the early work of Mrs. Eliot expresses the anguish and barrenness of modern life and the isolation of the individual.".

    a) expresses

    b) isolation

    c) Many

609. Choose the wrong word: "New universities are being establish at a slower rate nowadays due to the lack of federal and state funds.".

    a) slower

    b) due to the

    c) establish

610. Choose the wrong word: "Civil engineers had better planning to use steel supports in concrete structures built on unstable geophysical sites.".

    a) planning

    b) to use

    c) built

611. Choose the wrong word: "In the bag not only all her money but also all her keys were, none of which she got back.".

    a) not only

b) none of which

c) were

612. Choose the wrong word: "The contractings of the heart cause the blood to circulate.".

    a) heart

    b) contractings

    c) to circulate

613. Choose the wrong word: "Mr. Smith wrote the novel as a tribute to the Civil War soldiers who had laid on the battlefields and whom he had seen while serving as an army nurse.".

    a) had laid

    b) whom

    c) had seen

614. Choose the wrong word: "Because not food is as nutritious for a baby as its mother's milk, many women are returning to the practice of breast feeding.".

    a) as nutritious

    b) not food

    c) many

615. Choose the wrong word: "Who he decides to see and when what is the main cause of contention between Daniel and Sarah whose marriage is otherwise quite good.".

    a) between

    b) is otherwise

    c) when what is

616. Choose the wrong word: "The Nineteenth Amendment to the Constitution gives women the right to vote in the elections of 1920.".

    a) to vote

    b) gives

    c) the elections

617. Choose the wrong word: "The aims of the EEC are to eliminate tariffs between member countries; developing common policies for agriculture, labor, welfare, trade and transportation; and to abolish trusts and cartels.".

    a) to abolish

b) developing

c) are

618. Choose the wrong word: "Of the two Diomede Islands, only one belongs the United States.".

    a) belongs the

    b) the two

    c) Of

619. Choose the wrong word: "Moby-Dick is a novel that telling the story of a ship captain's single-minded hatred of a huge white whale.".

    a) novel

    b) single-minded

    c) telling

620. Choose the wrong word: "Please don't parking in those spaces that have sings reserving them for the handicapped.".

    a) don't parking

    b) reserving

    c) the handicapped

621. Choose the wrong word: "The more important theorem of all in plane geometry is the Pythagorean Theorem.".

    a) The

    b) more

    c) is

622. Choose the wrong word: "In additions to serving as a member of the President's Cabinet, the Attorney General is the head of the Justice Department.".

    a) serving as

    b) head

    c) In additions to

623. Choose the wrong word: "Despite of many attempts to introduce a universal language, notably Esperanto and Idiom Neutral, the effort has met with very little success.".

    a) Despite of

    b) many

    c) to introduce

624. Choose the wrong word: "Neither of the scout leaders know how to trap wild animals or how to prepare them for mounting.".

    a) of the

    b) know

    c) for mounting

625. Choose the wrong word: "Hardly he had entered the office when he realized that he had forgotten his wallet.".

    a) that he had

    b) forgotten

    c) Hardly he had

626. Choose the wrong word: "While searching for the wreckage of a unidentified aircraft, the Coast Guard encountered severe squeals at sea.".

    a) the

    b) a

    c) While searching

627. Choose the wrong word: "He has less friends in his classes now than he had last year.".

    a) less

    b) than

    c) last year

628. Choose the wrong word: "From now on new buildings in level one earthquake zones in the United States are to constructed to withstand a tremor without suffering damage.".

    a) From now on

    b) to constructed

    c) suffering

629. Choose the wrong word: "The native people of the Americans are called Indians because when Columbus landed in the Bahamas he thought that he has reached the East Indies.".

    a) are called

    b) has reached

    c) because

630. Choose the wrong word: "Daniel is one of the most intelligent boys of the science class.".

    a) of

b) most

c) science

631. Choose the wrong word: "Antibiotics can be convenience grouped according to the species of microorganisms they inhibit.".

    a) according

    b) species

    c) convenience

632. Choose the wrong word: "Daniel stopped to write his letter because he had to leave for the hospital.".

    a) because

    b) to write

    c) leave

633. Choose the wrong word: "If England had not imposed a tax on tea two hundred and twenty years ago, will the United States have remained part of the British Commonwealth?".

    a) will

    b) imposed

    c) ago

634. Choose the wrong word: "While they were away at the beach, they allowed their neighbors use their barbeque grill.".

    a) their neighbors

    b) While

    c) use

635. Choose the wrong word: "For a rattlesnake a dozen or so meals a year are quite suffience.".

    a) or so

    b) suffience

    c) are

636. Choose the wrong word: "He has been hoped for a raise for the last four months, but his boss is reluctant to give him one.".

    a) has been hoped

    b) last

    c) to give

637. Choose the wrong word: "She worked extensively during the second half of the nineteenth century to improve condition in mental health

facilities and the prisons.".
   a) during the
   b) extensively
   c) to improve condition

638. Choose the wrong word: "Mobile telephones have replaced the pagers as the most common accouterments of the up-to-date young businessperson.".
   a) the pagers
   b) most common
   c) up-to-date

639. Choose the wrong word: "Mosquitos are such fast breeders that it is almost impossible to control them either by draining areas where they breed or to spray them with pesticides.".
   a) such
   b) to spray
   c) they breed

640. Choose the wrong word: "The philanthropist did not feel sad when he donated his only to the museum.".
   a) did not
   b) when
   c) his only

641. Choose the wrong word: "In 1931 Mrs. Adams was a Nobel Prize recipient for she humanitarian achievements.".
   a) was
   b) she
   c) achievements

642. Choose the wrong word: "Carbohydrates and fats are two essential sources of energy for animal grow.".
   a) grow
   b) and fats
   c) sources

643. Choose the wrong word: "Located in the cranial cavity in the skull, the brain is the larger mass of nerve tissue in the human body.".
   a) the brain

b) human body

c) larger

644. Choose the wrong word: "The Pilgrims were 102 English emigrants whom, after arriving, became the first European settlers in New England.".

    a) whom

    b) became

    c) arriving

645. Choose the wrong word: "A turtle differs from all other reptiles in that its body is encased in a protective shell of their own.".

    a) from

    b) their

    c) own

646. Choose the wrong word: "There are no pouched animals in the United States but only the opossum.".

    a) There are

    b) no

    c) but only

647. Choose the wrong word: "For many years, scientists studying the effects that the sun has on human skin.".

    a) studying

    b) on human skin

    c) For

648. Choose the wrong word: "Gorillas live in largely permanently family groups like humans.".

    a) largely

    b) permanently

    c) like humans

649. Choose the wrong word: "Some birds, such as quails, can move instant from a resting position to full flight.".

    a) instant

    b) to

    c) resting

650. Choose the wrong word: "Radioactive dating is the accuratest method yet devised for determining the age of fossils.".

    a) is

b) method

c) for

651. Choose the wrong word: "The cobras when them strike raise themselves high above the ground on their tails and then fall forward.".

    a) raise

    b) fall forward

    c) them strike

652. Choose the wrong word: "The first professional baseball game it took place in 1846.".

    a) The first

    b) professional

    c) it

653. Choose the wrong word: "The statement will be spoken just one time; therefore, you must listen very careful in order to understand what the speaker has said.".

    a) very careful

    b) will be spoken

    c) what

654. Choose the wrong word: "Heat, left to their own devices, always flows from a given place to another place that is colder.".

    a) flows from

    b) their own devices

    c) that

655. Choose the wrong word: "The common field mouse is about four inches long and has a three-inched tail.".

    a) three-inched

    b) common

    c) long

656. Choose the wrong word: "Although almost all insects have six legs a immature insect may not have any.".

    a) a

    b) almost all

    c) have

657. Choose the wrong word: "Sloths spend most of its time hanging upside down from trees and feeding on leaves and fruit.".

a) most

b) feeding

c) fruit

658. Choose the wrong word: "In the relatively short history of industrial developing in this country, this city has played a vital role.".

a) relatively

b) developing

c) has played

659. Choose the wrong word: "Interest in automatic data processing has grown rapid since the first large calculators were introduced in 1950.".

a) rapid

b) grown

c) since

660. Choose the wrong word: "An ardent feminist, Mrs. Fuller, through her literature, asked that women be given a fairly chance.".

a) that

b) be

c) fairly

661. Choose the wrong word: "According to many educators, television should not become a replacement for good teachers, and neither are computers.".

a) According

b) many educators

c) are

662. Choose the wrong word: "According to Amazon legends, men were forced to do all of the household tasks for the women warriors who governed and protected the cities for they.".

a) for they

b) were forced

c) to do

663. Choose the wrong word: "The more the relative humidity reading rises, the worst the heat affects us.".

a) rises

b) the worst

c) affects

664. Choose the wrong word: "Because entertaining is such a competitive business, a group of singers or musicians needing a manager to help market the music.".

    a) Because

    b) such a competitive

    c) needing

665. Choose the wrong word: "Male guppies, like many other male fish, are more color than females.".

    a) Male

    b) color

    c) are

666. Choose the wrong word: "When children get their first pair of glasses, they are often surprise to see that trees and flowers have sharp clear outlines.".

    a) When

    b) pair

    c) surprise

667. Choose the wrong word: "Thunder that is audible from distances as far away as ten miles.".

    a) Thunder

    b) that

    c) miles

668. Choose the wrong word: "Advertising it provides most of the income for magazines, newspapers, radio and television in the UK today.".

    a) it

    b) provides

    c) most of the income

669. Choose the wrong word: "Many people say that California is a state of geographic remarkable diversity.".

    a) a state

    b) diversity

    c) geographic remarkable

670. Choose the wrong word: "The surface of the tongue covered with tiny taste buds.".

    a) covered

b) tiny

c) buds

671. Choose the wrong word: "Braille designed a form of communication enabling people to convey and preserve their thoughts to incorporate a series of dots which were read by the finger tips.".

a) to incorporate

b) enabling

c) were read

672. Choose the wrong word: "Underutilized species of fish has been proposed as a solution to the famine in many underdeveloped countries.".

a) to the famine

b) has been

c) Underutilized

673. Choose the wrong word: "The shore patrol has found the body of a man who they believe to be the missing marine biologist.".

a) has found

b) to be

c) who

674. Choose the wrong word: "The extent to which an individual is a product of either heredity or environment cannot proven, but several theories have been proposed.".

a) cannot proven

b) to which

c) several theories

675. Choose the wrong word: "Sex's education is instituted to help the student understand the process of maturation, to eliminate anxieties related to development and to prevent disease.".

a) Sex's education

b) related

c) to eliminate anxieties

676. Choose the wrong word: "Some bumper stickers are very funny and make us laugh, yet another can make us angry because of their ridiculousness.".

a) laugh

b) another

c) are

677. Choose the wrong word: "Several people have apparent tried to change the man's mind, but he refuses to listen.".

    a) have

    b) to listen

    c) apparent

678. Choose the wrong word: "Sometime ants keep smaller insects that give off honeydew, milking them regularly and even building barns to shelter them.".

    a) smaller insects

    b) Sometime

    c) to shelter

679. Choose the wrong word: "When the weather becomes colder we know that the air mass must originated in the Arctic rather than over the Gulf of Mexico.".

    a) must originated

    b) becomes

    c) colder

680. Choose the wrong word: "If his grades had been better, he would accept as a graduate student on the MBA program.".

    a) had been better

    b) the

    c) would accept

681. Choose the wrong word: "The Amish people would rather using horses than machines for transportation and farm work because they believe that a simple life keeps them closer to God.".

    a) using

    b) than

    c) farm work

682. Choose the wrong word: "Some of the rich have always ignored the less well-off and think they were a higher race.".

    a) Some of

    b) higher

    c) think

683. Choose the wrong word: "The poet Nash often used a comic style to do a serious point.".

    a) often used

    b) to do

    c) comic

684. Choose the wrong word: "Living in New York, apartments cost more to rent than they do in other smaller cities.".

    a) Living

    b) more

    c) smaller

685. Choose the wrong word: "Because the solar tiles were very secure fastened, only a few became detached when the Space Shuttle reentered the earth's atmosphere.".

    a) a few

    b) detached

    c) secure fastened

686. Choose the wrong word: "For a quarter of century, Mr. Maud was a compelling figure in this city's suffrage and labor movements.".

    a) a compelling

    b) of century

    c) labor

687. Choose the wrong word: "In the sixteenth century, Spain because involved in foreign wars with several other European countries and could not find the means of finance the battles that ensued.".

    a) of finance

    b) because involved

    c) several other

688. Choose the wrong word: "Writing of instructions for computers is called computer programming.".

    a) for

    b) called

    c) Writing of

689. Choose the wrong word: "Never before has so many people in the US been interested in soccer.".

    a) so many

b) has

c) interested in

690. Choose the wrong word: "According to some scientists, the earth losing its outer atmosphere because of pollutants.".

    a) losing

    b) its

    c) because of

691. Choose the wrong word: "Despite of the Hartley Act which forbids unfair union practices, some unions such as the air traffic controllers have voted to strike even though it might endanger the national security.".

    a) forbids

    b) to strike

    c) Despite of

692. Choose the wrong word: "His roommate is not very clever student but he certainly works very hard indeed.".

    a) not very

    b) but

    c) hard indeed

693. Choose the wrong word: "Until diamonds are cut and polished, they just like look small blue-grey stones.".

    a) cut and polished

    b) like look

    c) stones

694. Choose the wrong word: "Before creating the telegraph, Morse made their living as a painter.".

    a) their

    b) creating

    c) as

695. Choose the wrong word: "Prevented the soil from erosion. the trees planted by the farmer many years before were what stopped the flood from reaching his house.".

    a) before

    b) what

    c) Prevented

696. Choose the wrong word: "Since the average age of families has fallen, therefore more and more women have been able to join the labor force.".

    a) therefore

    b) have been

    c) the labor

697. Choose the wrong word: "Since lightning was probably significant in the formation of life, understanding it might help us to understanding life itself.".

    a) might

    b) help

    c) to understanding

698. Choose the wrong word: "The narwhal can be easily to recognize by the long spiraled tusk attached to the left side of its head.".

    a) spiraled

    b) its

    c) to recognize

699. Choose the wrong word: "In spite modern medical technology, many diseases caused by viruses are still not curable.".

    a) many

    b) In spite

    c) by viruses

700. Choose the wrong word: "Because national statistics on crime have only been kept for 1910, it is not possible to make judgments about crime during the early years of the nation.".

    a) for 1910

    b) to make

    c) early years

701. Choose the wrong word: "Some birds can travel at speeds approaching one hundred miles an hour, and a few land animals can so.".

    a) Some birds

    b) a few land animals

    c) so

702. Choose the wrong word: "Million of tourists from all over the world visit New York every year.".

    a) all over

b) visit

c) every

703. Choose the wrong word: "Some studies show that young babies prefer the smell of milk to those of other liquids.".

    a) smell

    b) those

    c) other liquids

704. Choose the wrong word: "The famous London Bridge, that is now gracing an American town, is by no means the most beautiful bridge in the world.".

    a) that

    b) most

    c) by no means

705. Choose the wrong word: "Since I started taking exercise every day, I found that not only am I fitter but I am also more alert.".

    a) taking

    b) am I

    c) found

706. Choose the wrong word: "For a long time, this officials have been known throughout the country as political bosses and law enforcers.".

    a) this

    b) have been known

    c) as

707. Choose the wrong word: "Although federal support for basic research programs are much less than it was ten years ago, more funds are now available from this foundation.".

    a) for

    b) are

    c) much

708. Choose the wrong word: "John Hancock was the first to do his signature on the Declaration of Independence.".

    a) the first

    b) do

    c) was

709. Choose the wrong word: "A sore throat interferes with daily life by making swallow difficult.".

    a) daily

    b) by

    c) swallow

710. Choose the wrong word: "Most American university degrees are awarded on completion of a specified amount of courses which earn students credits or points.".

    a) amount

    b) credits

    c) points

711. Choose the wrong word: "Fruit and vegetables supply few protein in relation to their weight and only a trace of fat.".

    a) vegetables

    b) few

    c) Fruit

712. Choose the wrong word: "According to the graduate catalog, student housing is more cheaper than housing off campus.".

    a) is

    b) According

    c) more cheaper

713. Choose the wrong word: "Of all the reference materials, the encyclopedia is the one that most people using.".

    a) using

    b) most

    c) is

714. Choose the wrong word: "In the spirit of the naturalist writers, that author's work portrays man's struggle for surviving.".

    a) naturalist

    b) In the spirit

    c) surviving

715. Choose the wrong word: "Scientific fish farming, known as aquaculture, has existed for more than 3000 years, but scientists who make research in this field are only recently providing relevant information.".

a) make
b) fish farming
c) field

716. Choose the wrong word: "It is the role of the National Bureau of Standards to establish accurate measurements for science, industrial and commerce.".
   a) establish
   b) industrial
   c) measurements

717. Choose the wrong word: "Of all the states in the US, Rhode island is the smallest.".
   a) in the
   b) all the
   c) is

718. Choose the wrong word: "Active animal life exists at all temperatures from the melting point of ice, 32 degree, to about 40 degree below boiling point of water.".
   a) boiling
   b) water
   c) the melting

719. Choose the wrong word: "After the team of geologists had drawn diagrams in their notebooks and wrote explanations of the formations which they had observed, they returned to their camp-side to compare notes.".
   a) which
   b) wrote
   c) their

720. Choose the wrong word: "The smallest of the apes, the gibbon, is distinguished by its too long arms.".
   a) The smallest
   b) too long
   c) its

721. Choose the wrong word: "When I last saw Sarah, she hurried to her next class on the other side of the campus and did not have time to talk.".
   a) hurried

b) I last

c) the other

722. Choose the wrong word: "The price of crude oil used to be a great deal lower than now, wasn't it?".

    a) price

    b) wasn't it

    c) lower

723. Choose the wrong word: "If one is invited out to a dinner, it is perfectly proper to go either with or without no a gift.".

    a) to go

    b) one

    c) no

724. Choose the wrong word: "Laser technology is the heart of a new generation of high-speed copiers and printer.".

    a) a

    b) printer

    c) generation

725. Choose the wrong word: "A manifest is an itemizing list of the goods or passengers a vessel is carrying.".

    a) itemizing

    b) of the goods

    c) is an

726. Choose the wrong word: "There was a very interesting news on the radio this morning about the earthquake in India.".

    a) a

    b) There was

    c) on the

727. Choose the wrong word: "He knows to repair the carburetor without taking the whole car apart.".

    a) the

    b) taking

    c) knows

728. Choose the wrong word: "On February 20, 1968 this spaceship orbiting the earth in a manned flight that lasted just under five hours.".

    a) manned

b) orbiting

c) just under

729. Choose the wrong word: "Although it can be closely nearly approached, absolute zero cannot be reached experimentally.".

    a) it can

    b) closely nearly

    c) be reached

730. Choose the wrong word: "Mr. Robinson, whose joined the team in 2004, was the first black American to play baseball in the major leagues.".

    a) whose

    b) was

    c) to play

731. Choose the wrong word: "It is said that Einstein felt very badly about the application of his theories to the creation of weapons of war.".

    a) It is said

    b) very

    c) badly

732. Choose the wrong word: "The state of New Mexico is not densely population, with an average of only four people per square kilometer.".

    a) is not

    b) with an

    c) population

733. Choose the wrong word: "The virtues of ordinary life is the focus of many poems.".

    a) The

    b) is

    c) ordinary

734. Choose the wrong word: "Absolute zero, the temperature at whom all substances have zero thermal energy and thus, the lowest possible temperatures, is unattainable in practice.".

    a) all substances

    b) whom

    c) is

735. Choose the wrong word: "Not single alphabet has ever perfectly represented the sounds of any of Earth's natural languages.".

a) Not

b) sounds

c) any of

736. Choose the wrong word: "New synthetic materials have improved the construction of artificial body parts by provide both the power and the range of action for a natural limb.".

    a) body parts

    b) provide

    c) have

737. Choose the wrong word: "The Earth depends the sun for its heating.".

    a) sun for

    b) heating

    c) depends

738. Choose the wrong word: "Perhaps the colonists were looking for a climate like England, when they decided to settle the North American continent.".

    a) looking for

    b) like England

    c) to settle

739. Choose the wrong word: "Chicago, is called the Windy City because of the winds coming down across the lake from Canada, is never very hot in summer.".

    a) because of

    b) never very

    c) Chicago, is called

740. Choose the wrong word: "Although no country has exactly the same folk music like that of any other, it is significant that similar song exist among widely separated people.".

    a) no country

    b) like

    c) widely

741. Choose the wrong word: "First raise your right hand, and then you should repeat after me.".

    a) you should

b) and then

c) after me

742. Choose the wrong word: "The journey by train is more short but more expensive and definitely more comfortable than by bus.".
    a) more short
    b) but
    c) definitely

743. Choose the wrong word: "An X-ray microscope enables a person to see on solid materials such as metal and bone.".
    a) enables
    b) such as
    c) on

744. Choose the wrong word: "Dairying is concerned not only with the production of milk but with the manufacture of milk products such as butter and cheese.".
    a) is
    b) with
    c) but

745. Choose the wrong word: "The body temperature of cold-blooded animal is varying with that of its environment and may reach a temperature of above 9 degree in the sun.".
    a) that
    b) is varying
    c) may reach

746. Choose the wrong word: "The biologist found some pollutants, a little of which can be considered very harmful to fish and other living organisms, in the river.".
    a) be considered
    b) fish
    c) a little

747. Choose the wrong word: "A future system of solid waste managements should begin with reduction in the amount of waste.".
    a) managements
    b) reduction
    c) solid

748. Choose the wrong word: "How many people know that this bridge, built in 1983, were the world's first suspension bridge?".

    a) many

    b) were

    c) built

749. Choose the wrong word: "In order to get married in this state, one must present a medical report along with your identification.".

    a) In order to

    b) along with

    c) your

750. Choose the wrong word: "The famous man won both the pentathlon or decathlon in the 1912 Olympic Games.".

    a) or

    b) won

    c) in

751. Choose the wrong word: "Daniel was upset last night because he had to do too many home works.".

    a) upset

    b) many home works

    c) had to do

752. Choose the wrong word: "They are known that colds can be avoided by eating the right kind of food and taking exercise regularly.".

    a) They are known

    b) be avoided

    c) by

753. Choose the wrong word: "With American prices for sugar at three times as much the world price, manufacturers are beginning to use fructose blended with pure sugar, or sucrose.".

    a) are

    b) to use

    c) as much

754. Choose the wrong word: "A university professor reported that he discovers a vaccine which has been 80 percent effective in reducing the instances of tooth decay among small children.".

    a) which

b) discovers

c) among

755. Choose the wrong word: "Find in 1953, this newspaper was the first successful penny newspaper.".

    a) Find

    b) the first

    c) newspaper

756. Choose the wrong word: "The state with the most large production of tobacco products in North Carolina.".

    a) with the

    b) products

    c) most large

757. Choose the wrong word: "The shortest route for the rally drivers was through the mountains whereas if the desert road was much longer though faster.".

    a) through

    b) much

    c) whereas if

758. Choose the wrong word: "The problems which beset the first settlers were nothing compared to those which faced the lately ones who landed further north.".

    a) nothing

    b) the lately ones

    c) beset

759. Choose the wrong word: "Starfishes and sea urchins are particularly interested because of their unusual structures.".

    a) interested

    b) because of

    c) are

760. Choose the wrong word: "Electric telegraph invented in 1835 by Mr. Morse, was first used in 1844.".

    a) first

    b) used

    c) Electric telegraph

761. Choose the wrong word: "Before the Industrial Revolution come to America, the vast majority of the population lived in rural areas.".
    a) come to
    b) Before the
    c) lived

762. Choose the wrong word: "Certain bats used their own sound to locate foods and to avoid obstacles as they fly at night.".
    a) and to avoid
    b) used
    c) to locate

763. Choose the wrong word: "The audible range of frequencies for human beings usually lays between 20 and 20,000 Hz.".
    a) for
    b) between
    c) lays

764. Choose the wrong word: "Hay fever symptoms, ranged from mild to severe, differ in degree according to the individual.".
    a) ranged
    b) to
    c) differ

765. Choose the wrong word: "Many people have stopped to smoke because they are afraid that it may be harmful to their health.".
    a) because
    b) may be
    c) to smoke

766. Choose the wrong word: "In purchasing a winter coat, it is very important for trying it on with heavy clothing underneath.".
    a) very
    b) for trying
    c) In purchasing

767. Choose the wrong word: "She wishes that we didn't send her the candy yesterday because she's on a diet.".
    a) the candy
    b) because
    c) didn't send her

768. Choose the wrong word: "Nitrogen must be combine with another element such as hydrogen or oxygen to be useful in agriculture or industry.".

      a) must be combine

      b) another element

      c) such as

769. Choose the wrong word: "Please send me information with regard of insurance policies available from your company.".

      a) insurance

      b) from

      c) with regard of

770. Choose the wrong word: "Her best known role of Mrs. Garland was as Dorothy in The Wizard of Oz.".

      a) Her

      b) best

      c) role

771. Choose the wrong word: "The school board decided to suspend the new teacher who late to proctor the final examination.".

      a) decided

      b) late

      c) the final

772. Choose the wrong word: "In spite of her physician handicaps, she graduated from Radcliffe with honors.".

      a) In spite of

      b) from

      c) physician

773. Choose the wrong word: "Awards were given to the best athletes, sportsmen and coaches at the annual dinner of the Association.".

      a) were given

      b) sportsmen and coaches

      c) annual

774. Choose the wrong word: "Industrial lasers are most often used for cutting, welding, drilling and measure.".

      a) measure

b) most often

c) Industrial

775. Choose the wrong word: "As a young man, Darwin showed little promising as a biologist.".
    a) showed
    b) a biologist
    c) promising

776. Choose the wrong word: "Fewest than half of all adults fully understand the kinds and amounts of exercise necessary for an effective physical fitness program.".
    a) adults
    b) kinds
    c) Fewest

777. Choose the wrong word: "Had we known the traffic would be so bad, we did not drive back from work so early.".
    a) be
    b) Had we known
    c) did not drive

778. Choose the wrong word: "The student realised with disappointment that he had learned new nothing in the lecture.".
    a) with
    b) new nothing
    c) that

779. Choose the wrong word: "According the kinetic theory, all mater consists of constantly moving particles.".
    a) moving
    b) According the
    c) consists

780. Choose the wrong word: "Mr. Faulkner said that it is not possible to understand the South unless you were born there.".
    a) to understand
    b) you
    c) is

781. Choose the wrong word: "It is generally believed that Thomas Jefferson was the one who had researched and wrote the Declaration of

Independence.".
a) wrote
b) its signing
c) It is generally believed

782. Choose the wrong word: "The bridge at Niagara Falls spans the longer unguarded border in the history of the world, symbolizing the peace and goodwill that exist between Canada and the US.".
a) exist
b) between
c) the longer

783. Choose the wrong word: "The two types of nucleic acids, known as DNA and RNA, are not the alike.".
a) known
b) the alike
c) types of

784. Choose the wrong word: "People who speak to theirselves are not necessarily disturbed, but according to one leading psychologist merely doing what we would all do if we could.".
a) theirselves
b) speak
c) what we

785. Choose the wrong word: "Mike has worked in three different companies in three different positions, so he has more work experience than the other applicant's.".
a) has
b) in
c) the other applicant's

786. Choose the wrong word: "Alike bases which cause litmus to turn blue, acids cause litmus to turn red.".
a) Alike
b) which
c) acids

787. Choose the wrong word: "Until the project completed, the effects of the new measures will not be known, especially in rural areas.".
a) Until

b) completed

c) effects

788. Choose the wrong word: "Only a little early scientists among them Bacon, Copernicus and Bruno, believed that the principles underlying the physical world could be discovered and understood through careful observation and analysis.".

    a) among

    b) the principles

    c) Only a little early scientists

789. Choose the wrong word: "Cholesterol help the body by making hormones and building cell walls, but too much cholesterol can cause heart problems.".

    a) by making

    b) help

    c) too much

790. Choose the wrong word: "Accountants are always busy on April because both federal and state taxes are due on the fifteenth.".

    a) on April

    b) and

    c) on the fifteenth

791. Choose the wrong word: "Hummingbirds are the only birds capable to fly backward as well as forward, up and down.".

    a) the only birds

    b) to fly

    c) as well as

792. Choose the wrong word: "Neon is often used in airplane beacons because neon beacons are very visible that they can be seen even through dense fog.".

    a) is often

    b) they

    c) very

793. Choose the wrong word: "In the 1840s, hundreds of families pioneer moved west in their covered wagons.".

    a) families pioneer

b) hundreds

c) In the

794. Choose the wrong word: "The United States has a younger population as most other major industrial countries.".

    a) has

    b) countries

    c) as

795. Choose the wrong word: "When an university formulates new regulations, it must relay its decision to the students and faculty.".

    a) an

    b) regulations

    c) must relay

796. Choose the wrong word: "Although jogging is a good way to lose weight and improve one's physical condition, most doctors recommend that the potential jogger begin in a correct manner by getting a complete checkup.".

    a) jogging

    b) in a correct manner

    c) most

797. Choose the wrong word: "Urban consumers have formed co-operatives to provide themselves with necessities such groceries, household appliances, and gasoline at a lower cost.".

    a) have formed

    b) to provide

    c) such

798. Choose the wrong word: "The first electric lamp had two carbon rods from which vapor serves to conduct the current across the gap.".

    a) The first

    b) which

    c) serves

799. Choose the wrong word: "The American buffalo must be reproduce itself again because it has been removed from the endangered species list.".

    a) itself

b) reproduce

c) because

800. Choose the wrong word: "Once the scientist had figured out the precise path of the comet, he is finding that he was able to predict its next appearance.".

    a) is finding

    b) Once

    c) to predict

801. Choose the wrong word: "There are a large supply of pens and notebooks in the storeroom to the left of the library entrance.".

    a) of pens

    b) to the left of

    c) are

802. Choose the wrong word: "Soon after the United States' entrance into the war the major hotels was transformed into military barracks.".

    a) was

    b) Soon after

    c) entrance

803. Choose the wrong word: "From the vibrations of the web, was set up by trapped animal, a spider learns much about nature of its catch.".

    a) was set up

    b) learns

    c) trapped animal

804. Choose the wrong word: "Because a felony is more bad than a misdemeanor, the punishment is more severe, and often includes a jail sentence as well as a fine.".

    a) more severe

    b) more bad

    c) as well as

805. Choose the wrong word: "The Board of Realtors doesn't have any informations about the increase in rent for this area.".

    a) about

    b) increase

    c) informations

806. Choose the wrong word: "The amount of copper sulfate used in the experiment depends from the intensity of the heat.".

    a) amount

    b) from

    c) the heat

807. Choose the wrong word: "The actress was supposed to should attend the film premier but she became ill at the last moment.".

    a) was

    b) became

    c) should attend

808. Choose the wrong word: "Mr. Franklin, as an inventor, he had broad interests, mechanical skills, persistence and a practical view of life.".

    a) as an

    b) he

    c) persistence

809. Choose the wrong word: "According to the experts, genetic inheritance is probability the most important factor in determining a person's health.".

    a) probability

    b) genetic

    c) the most

810. Choose the wrong word: "Because of their expedition, the United States begin to realize the true value of the territory.".

    a) begin

    b) the true value

    c) territory

811. Choose the wrong word: "The purchased of this building was one of the biggest events in the history of the company.".

    a) was

    b) events

    c) purchased

812. Choose the wrong word: "Since the early years of this century people has flown across oceans to test their machines, test themselves and respond to their craving for adventure.".

    a) has flown

b) Since

c) test

813. Choose the wrong word: "The idea of a submarine is an old ancient one, dating from as early as the fifteenth century.".

    a) as early as

    b) century

    c) an old ancient one

814. Choose the wrong word: "Philosophy, the inquiry into the nature of human knowledge, it is still a popular subject among university students.".

    a) into the nature of

    b) it is

    c) among

815. Choose the wrong word: "This road is call the High Road because it is at an altitude of 5,300 feet.".

    a) call

    b) it is

    c) an altitude

816. Choose the wrong word: "Both cattle or railroads helped build the city of Chicago.".

    a) cattle

    b) or

    c) build

817. Choose the wrong word: "He founded a base at Port Royal in 1605 and builds a fort at Quebec three years later.".

    a) founded

    b) at Quebec

    c) builds

818. Choose the wrong word: "The term "Vitamine" is proposed by Casimir Funk, who suspected that these substances were essential for life.".

    a) is proposed by

    b) who suspected

    c) were

819. Choose the wrong word: "A progress has been made toward finding a cure for AIDS.".

a) has been made

b) A progress

c) a cure

820. Choose the wrong word: "Too much water makes plants turning brown on the edges of their leaves.".

    a) makes

    b) their

    c) turning

821. Choose the wrong word: "Patients suffering from encephalitis have an inflammatory of the brain.".

    a) from

    b) suffering

    c) inflammatory

822. Choose the wrong word: "As television images of the astronauts showed, even for trained professionals who are used to move about in a lessened gravitational field, there are still problems.".

    a) As

    b) used to move

    c) there are

823. Choose the wrong word: "These universities bear the name of their state, and its achievements are recognized as state achievements.".

    a) its

    b) bear

    c) their

824. Choose the wrong word: "In 1961 America's first manned spacecraft launched.".

    a) manned

    b) launched

    c) In

825. Choose the wrong word: "The tongue is the principle organ of taste, and is crucial for chewing, swallowed and speaking.".

    a) swallowed

    b) of taste

    c) principle

826. Choose the wrong word: "African-American quilts are lively and spontaneously, but unlike jazz, the quilts are just now starting to receive recognition.".

    a) unlike

    b) just

    c) spontaneously

827. Choose the wrong word: "Some jellyfish make daily journeys from deep water to the surface and back, while others migrate horizontal.".

    a) make

    b) horizontal

    c) from deep

828. Choose the wrong word: "The concept of lift in aerodynamics refers to the relationship among the increased speed of air over the top of a wing and the higher pressure of the slower air underneath.".

    a) refers to

    b) increased

    c) among

829. Choose the wrong word: "A few tiles on Skylab were the only equipments that failed to perform well in outer space.".

    a) equipments

    b) A few

    c) were

830. Choose the wrong word: "Although he was happily married he preferred spending lately hours at work to spending evenings lazily at home.".

    a) happily

    b) to spending

    c) lately

831. Choose the wrong word: "Only once before this century a comet as big as this one had come so close to the Earth.".

    a) one

    b) so

    c) had

832. Choose the wrong word: "Each salmon remember the precise taste of the water in which it hatched.".

a) remember

b) the precise

c) it

833. Choose the wrong word: "Sarah had better to change her study habits if she hopes to be admitted to a good university.".

a) to a good university

b) hopes to be

c) to change

834. Choose the wrong word: "Doctors agree that the fluid around the spinal cord helps the nourish the brain.".

a) the fluid

b) the nourish

c) Doctors

835. Choose the wrong word: "Forgetting something usually mean an inability to retrieve the material that is still stored somewhere in the memory.".

a) usually

b) is

c) mean

836. Choose the wrong word: "Some executives require that the secretary is responsible for writing all reports as well as for balancing the books.".

a) is

b) that

c) writing

837. Choose the wrong word: "Philosophy of the ancient Greeks has been preserved in the scholarly writing of Western civilization.".

a) has been preserved

b) Philosophy

c) scholarly

838. Choose the wrong word: "Most large corporations provide pension plans for their employees so that they will be secure enough than to live comfortably during their retirement.".

a) secure enough than

b) so that

c) to live

839. Choose the wrong word: "They are planning on attending the convention next month, and so I am.".
    a) next
    b) attending
    c) so I am

840. Choose the wrong word: "Benjamin Franklin's ability to learn from observation and experience contributed greatly to him success in public life.".
    a) ability
    b) him
    c) in

841. Choose the wrong word: "The new system responds at seconds to any emergency.".
    a) The
    b) at
    c) any

842. Choose the wrong word: "The diesel engine that runs on oil is efficient than most other engines because it converts more of the useful energy stored up in the fuel.".
    a) efficient
    b) that
    c) is

843. Choose the wrong word: "The area where a microchip is manufactured must be the most cleanest environment possible.".
    a) a microchip
    b) be
    c) most cleanest

844. Choose the wrong word: "The new student was consistently correct in Math quizzes all the time, which pleased the teacher but not us.".
    a) The new
    b) which
    c) all the time

845. Choose the wrong word: "The side of the pupil, according to psychologists, is effected by mental activity.".
    a) mental activity

b) is effected

c) according to

846. Choose the wrong word: "The main office of the factory can be found in Maple Street in Boston.".

    a) in

    b) be found

    c) The main

847. Choose the wrong word: "The instructor advised the students for the procedures to follow in writing the term paper.".

    a) follow

    b) in writing

    c) for

848. Choose the wrong word: "The government requires that a census be taken every ten years so accurate statistics may be compiled.".

    a) be taken

    b) so

    c) every ten years

849. Choose the wrong word: "Even though they conceived the idea of natural selection at the same time, Darwin was credited because his earlier papers.".

    a) was credited

    b) conceived

    c) because

850. Choose the wrong word: "Freshman students are encouraged to take part in sports such as football, basketball and to ride.".

    a) to ride

    b) sports

    c) are encouraged

851. Choose the wrong word: "It is believed that a people could live on Mars with little life support because the atmosphere is similar to that of Earth.".

    a) live

    b) that

    c) a people

852. Choose the wrong word: "Boys cannot become Cub Scouts unless completed the first grade.".
    a) the first grade
    b) unless completed
    c) become

853. Choose the wrong word: "More than 300 different kinds of nails is manufactured in the United States.".
    a) kinds
    b) is
    c) More than

854. Choose the wrong word: "Landscape painting a dominant art forms during much of the nineteenth century.".
    a) painting
    b) during
    c) forms

855. Choose the wrong word: "An organ is a group of tissues capable to perform some special function, as for example, the heart, the liver or the lungs.".
    a) to perform
    b) for example
    c) of tissues

856. Choose the wrong word: "Sharks, when the current are in their favor, can smell blood issuing from a body at a distance of nearly half a kilometer.".
    a) their favor
    b) are
    c) issuing from

857. Choose the wrong word: "The 1890s in America were known as a Gay Nineties.".
    a) a
    b) as
    c) The

858. Choose the wrong word: "The need to improve technique motivates ballerinas exercising and rehearse for hours daily.".
    a) to improve

b) daily

c) exercising

859. Choose the wrong word: "After driving for twenty miles, he suddenly realized that he has been driving in the wrong direction.".

    a) realized

    b) has been driving

    c) in

860. Choose the wrong word: "Unexploded bombs buried deep in the ground have been found in the construction site opposite of the City Hall.".

    a) opposite of

    b) buried deep

    c) have been

861. Choose the wrong word: "The sun is a huge fiery globe at a average distance of 93,000,000 miles from the Earth.".

    a) fiery globe

    b) from

    c) a

862. Choose the wrong word: "Most modern observatories contain telescopes that scientists using as cameras to take photographs of remote galaxies.".

    a) Most

    b) using

    c) contain

863. Choose the wrong word: "Regardless of your teaching method, the objective of any conversation class should be for the students to practice speaking words.".

    a) speaking words

    b) should be

    c) Regardless of

864. Choose the wrong word: "Unlike light from other sources, which travels in direction, the light from a laser is highly directional.".

    a) Unlike

    b) which

    c) direction

865. Choose the wrong word: "There were so much people trying to leave the burning building that the police had a great deal of trouble controlling them.".

    a) much

    b) There were

    c) the burning

866. Choose the wrong word: "When a pregnant woman smokes, the blood supply to the uterus is affected, reduction oxygen to the fetus.".

    a) blood supply

    b) reduction

    c) affected

867. Choose the wrong word: "The teacher taught her students to look careful to the left and the right at least three times before crossing the highway.".

    a) careful

    b) taught

    c) to the

868. Choose the wrong word: "Increasing involvement in agriculture by large corporations has resulted in what is known as agribusiness. That is, agriculture with business techniques, heavy capitalization and to control all stages of the operations.".

    a) to control

    b) known as

    c) has resulted in

869. Choose the wrong word: "I would of attended the meeting of the planning committee last week, but I had to deliver a speech at a convention.".

    a) I had to deliver

    b) at a convention

    c) I would of

870. Choose the wrong word: "An alligator is an animal some like a crocodile, but with a broad, flattened snout.".

    a) some

    b) an animal

    c) flattened

871. Choose the wrong word: "The USS Richard was commanded by John Jones, that won a notable sea battle during the Revolution.".

    a) was
    b) that
    c) a notable

872. Choose the wrong word: "Many plant varieties, including most orchids and many of our trees and shrubs have little or no root hairs.".

    a) Many
    b) hairs
    c) little

873. Choose the wrong word: "Lectures for the next week will include the following: The Causes of the Civil War, The Economy of the North and Assassinating Lincoln.".

    a) for
    b) will include
    c) Assassinating

874. Choose the wrong word: "People in the world differ in his beliefs about the cause of sickness and health.".

    a) his
    b) differ
    c) about

875. Choose the wrong word: "As the demand increases, manufacturers who previously produced only a large, luxury car is compelled to make a smaller model in order to compete in the market.".

    a) previously
    b) is
    c) to make

876. Choose the wrong word: "When mining for gold, you must first obtain the gold ore and then apart the gold from the ore.".

    a) apart
    b) must first
    c) and then

877. Choose the wrong word: "Cotton fiber, like other vegetable fibers, are composed mostly of cellulose.".

    a) like

b) other

c) are

878. Choose the wrong word: "That it is believed that most of the earthquakes in the world occur near the youngest mountain ranges: the Himalayas and the Andes.".

    a) most of the earthquakes

    b) That it is believed

    c) the youngest

879. Choose the wrong word: "A barometer is a device with a sealed metal chamber designed to reading the changes in the pressure of air in the atmosphere.".

    a) reading

    b) A barometer

    c) reading

880. Choose the wrong word: "The understanding electricity depends on a knowledge of atoms and the subatomic particles of which they are composed.".

    a) depends on

    b) they

    c) The understanding

881. Choose the wrong word: "Gamma globulin, a protein found in blood plasma, it is used to prevent such infectious disease as measles and viral hepatitis.".

    a) such

    b) found in

    c) it is

882. Choose the wrong word: "Vasco da Gama, accompanied by a large crew and a fleet of twenty ships, were trying to establish Portuguese domination in Africa and India.".

    a) were

    b) to establish

    c) by a large crew

883. Choose the wrong word: "How much times did Daniel and Sarah have to do the experiment before they obtained the results they had been expecting.".

a) been expecting

b) much

c) obtained the results

884. Choose the wrong word: "There is no limit to the diversity to be finding in the cultures of people throughout the world.".

    a) cultures

    b) people

    c) finding

885. Choose the wrong word: "Scientific students should study how to use a computer as well as their own subject.".

    a) should

    b) Scientific

    c) their

886. Choose the wrong word: "When the silkworm gets through to lay its eggs, it dies.".

    a) to lay

    b) it dies

    c) its

887. Choose the wrong word: "A prism is used to refract white light so it spreads out in a continuous spectrum of colors.".

    a) it

    b) so

    c) to refract

888. Choose the wrong word: "Ozone has his origin in a number of sources, a prime one being the automobile engine.".

    a) prime

    b) being

    c) his

889. Choose the wrong word: "Latent learning is the association of indifferent stimuli or situations with one the other without reward.".

    a) the other

    b) or situations

    c) learning

890. Choose the wrong word: "Steven was very late getting home last night, and unfortunately for him, the dog barking woke everyone up.".

a) getting

b) dog

c) for him

891. Choose the wrong word: "A huge winter storm has brought the snow to Northern California's mountain counties.".

a) huge

b) counties

c) the

892. Choose the wrong word: "Almost American Indian culture have been agricultural societies since 2000 B.C.".

a) Almost

b) since

c) have been

893. Choose the wrong word: "Because the torrential rains that had devastated the area, the governor sent the National Guard to assist in the clean-up operation.".

a) torrential

b) Because

c) to assist in

894. Choose the wrong word: "The bridge was hitting by a large ship during a sudden storm last week.".

a) was hitting

b) during

c) sudden

895. Choose the wrong word: "The rate of the heartbeat have been controlling by a small node of nerve-like muscle tissue called the pacemaker.".

a) The rate of

b) have been controlling

c) the

896. Choose the wrong word: "Some important characteristics of the Baroque style was a renewed interest in ornamentation and a powerful use of both light and shade.".

a) use

b) and

c) was

897. Choose the wrong word: "Alexander Bell was once a teacher who run a school for the deaf in this city.".

    a) once

    b) run

    c) in

898. Choose the wrong word: "There exists more than 2,500 different varieties of palm trees, with varying flowers, leaves and fruits.".

    a) more than

    b) exists

    c) with

899. Choose the wrong word: "Ghost towns like this one are communities that are not longer inhabited because changes in economic conditions have caused people to move elsewhere.".

    a) not longer

    b) like

    c) because

900. Choose the wrong word: "Harry seldom pays his bills on time, and his brother does too.".

    a) does too

    b) on time

    c) his

901. Choose the wrong word: "Schizophrenia may be triggered by genetic predisposition, stressful, drugs or infections.".

    a) triggered

    b) genetic

    c) stressful

902. Choose the wrong word: "Many roads and railroad were built in the 1880s because of the industrial cities needed a network to link them with sources of supply.".

    a) were built

    b) because of

    c) to link

903. Choose the wrong word: "To building their nests, tailorbirds use their bills as needles.".
    a) nests
    b) their
    c) building

904. Choose the wrong word: "The only bird know to shine at night is the barn owl of Western Europe, which actually shines through a fungus sticking to their feathers.".
    a) their feathers
    b) shines
    c) which

905. Choose the wrong word: "According to the decision by the Supreme Court, an university may not use admissions quotas to obtain a racially balanced student body.".
    a) an
    b) use
    c) quotas

906. Choose the wrong word: "People who live in small towns often seem more warm and friendly than people who live in populated densely areas.".
    a) small towns
    b) populated densely
    c) who

907. Choose the wrong word: "The manager thought the new clerk was not a honest person so he set a trap for her.".
    a) a
    b) a trap
    c) for

908. Choose the wrong word: "The first vaccine ever developed was used to combat and fight a smallpox, a disease resulting from infection by a virus.".
    a) resulting from
    b) was used
    c) and fight a

909. Choose the wrong word: "My cousin composes not only the music, but also sings the songs for the band.".
   a) but
   b) composes not only
   c) major

910. Choose the wrong word: "I suggest that he goes to the doctor as soon as he returns from taking the exam.".
   a) goes
   b) that
   c) to the doctor

911. Choose the wrong word: "Despite the metric system is used throughout the world, it is still not commonly used in the United States.".
   a) Despite
   b) is used
   c) is still

912. Choose the wrong word: "This city is among the few cities in the country which has been awarded official status of a bilingual municipality.".
   a) among
   b) which
   c) has been awarded

913. Choose the wrong word: "The news of the president's treaty negotiations with the foreign government were received with mixed emotions by the citizens of both governments.".
   a) of both governments
   b) The
   c) were

914. Choose the wrong word: "Programs such as this one were developed to prepare children from deprived situations to enter school without to experience unusual difficulties.".
   a) such as
   b) without to experience
   c) to prepare

915. Choose the wrong word: "Harvard University was established just after sixteenth years they arrived.".

a) arrived

b) was

c) after sixteenth years

916. Choose the wrong word: "The guide told the tourists that it was a good restaurant specializing in seafood just round the corner from the museum.".

a) just round

b) it was a

c) specializing

917. Choose the wrong word: "Balloons have been used in various wars not only to direct artillery fire and report troop movements however to carry bombs and protect against low-flying planes.".

a) however

b) various wars

c) movements

918. Choose the wrong word: "During the early part of the Colonial period, living conditions were hard, and people have had little time for reading and studying.".

a) studying

b) people have had

c) were

919. Choose the wrong word: "They are famous for their beautiful art work, especially handmade jewelry cast from silver, carved from stones or decorations with beads and feathers.".

a) art work

b) especially

c) decorations

920. Choose the wrong word: "Although both of them are trying to get the scholarship, she has the highest grades.".

a) highest

b) of them

c) are trying

921. Choose the wrong word: "Until his last class at the university in 2010, Dave always turns in all of his assignments on time.".

a) Until

b) turns

c) of

922. Choose the wrong word: "Because of the approaching storm, the wind began to blow hard and the sky became dark as evening.".

    a) hard

    b) to blow

    c) as

923. Choose the wrong word: "The artist tried simulate interest in painting by taking his students to the museum.".

    a) interest in

    b) stimulate

    c) by taking

924. Choose the wrong word: "Marry being chosen as the most outstanding students of her campus made her parents very happy.".

    a) Marry

    b) chosen

    c) most outstanding

925. Choose the wrong word: "Mr. Peters used to think of hisself as the only president of the company.".

    a) think

    b) as the only

    c) hisself

926. Choose the wrong word: "Factoring is the process of finding two or more expressions whose product is equal as the given expression.".

    a) finding

    b) equal as

    c) whose

927. Choose the wrong word: "Sodium, usually a metal, and chlorine, usually a gas, they react to form the solid sodium chloride, or table salt.".

    a) they

    b) to form

    c) table salt

928. Choose the wrong word: "No longer is scientific discovery a matter of one person alone working.".

    a) No

b) matter of

c) alone working

929. Choose the wrong word: "The Alaskan malamute, used extensively for pulling sleds, is closely related about the wolf.".

    a) about

    b) for pulling

    c) used

930. Choose the wrong word: "His secretary called inform us he would be late for the meeting.".

    a) would be

    b) inform

    c) late

931. Choose the wrong word: "She must retyping the report, before she hands it in to the director of financing.".

    a) before

    b) hands it in

    c) retyping

932. Choose the wrong word: "A dam stops the flow of water, creating a reservoir and raise the level of water.".

    a) stops

    b) raise

    c) of water

933. Choose the wrong word: "Professional medical schools were organized in the 1780s and surgery made major gains when anesthetics was perfected in the 1840s.".

    a) was perfected

    b) made

    c) were organized

934. Choose the wrong word: "Not only Kingsley House Settlement nor all phases of the civic life of the city keenly interested her.".

    a) nor all

    b) keenly

    c) civic life

935. Choose the wrong word: "It may be argued that modern presidents have far great responsibilities than their predecessors did.".

a) argued

b) did

c) great

936. Choose the wrong word: "Most Americans would not be happy without a color television, two cars and working at an extra job.".

    a) Most

    b) working at

    c) without

937. Choose the wrong word: "The Department of Architecture has been criticized for not having much required courses scheduled for this semester.".

    a) much

    b) not having

    c) for

938. Choose the wrong word: "Despite of the fact that backgammon is easy to learn, it is as difficult to play as chess.".

    a) to play

    b) as chess

    c) Despite of

939. Choose the wrong word: "Those of us who smoke should have their lungs X-rayed regularly.".

    a) Those

    b) who

    c) their

940. Choose the wrong word: "Mr. Roosevelt demonstrated his competitive spirit and tireless energy in 1905 whenever he led the team up San Juan Hill.".

    a) demonstrated

    b) whenever

    c) competitive

941. Choose the wrong word: "The GATT is an international agreement designing to increase trade among member nations.".

    a) among

    b) designing

    c) international

942. Choose the wrong word: "Mr. Calder, who was originally interested in mechanical engineering, later became a sculpture.".

    a) sculpture

    b) originally

    c) later

943. Choose the wrong word: "Writers and media personnel sell theirselves best by the impression given in their verbal expression.".

    a) personnel

    b) by the

    c) theirselves

944. Choose the wrong word: "All the scouts got theirselves ready for the long camping trip by spending their weekends living in the open.".

    a) all

    b) theirselves

    c) living

945. Choose the wrong word: "Cosmic distance is measured on light-years.".

    a) on

    b) Cosmic

    c) years

946. Choose the wrong word: "Among Thomas Jefferson's many accomplishment was his work to establish this university.".

    a) Among

    b) to establish

    c) accomplishment

947. Choose the wrong word: "The registrar has requested that each student and teacher sign their name on the grade sheet before submitting it.".

    a) submitting

    b) their name

    c) sign

948. Choose the wrong word: "As Mrs. Bergman lived a life of courage, she also approached die with courage.".

    a) a life

b) die

c) As

949. Choose the wrong word: "The test administrator ordered we not to open our books until he told us to do so.".

    a) we

    b) not to open

    c) told us to do so

950. Choose the wrong word: "Everyone who has traveled across the US by car, train or bus are surprised to see such a large expanse of territory.".

    a) by

    b) who

    c) are

951. Choose the wrong word: "The Civil War was not only disastrous in terms of loss of human life but in the effects on the agriculture in the South.".

    a) but

    b) in terms of

    c) loss

952. Choose the wrong word: "The price at The Economy Center are as reasonable, if not more reasonable, as those at comparable discount stores.".

    a) if not more

    b) price

    c) discount

953. Choose the wrong word: "The brothers Grimm intended their fairy tales to be studied by scholars of German literature and not to enjoy as simple stories by children.".

    a) intended

    b) as simple

    c) to enjoy

954. Choose the wrong word: "There is an unresolved controversy as to whom is the real author of the Elizabethan plays commonly credited to Mr. Shakespeare.".

    a) whom

b) There is

c) commonly

955. Choose the wrong word: "In his early days as a direct, Charlie Chaplin produced 62 short, silent comedy films in four years.".

    a) his

    b) direct

    c) in four

956. Choose the wrong word: "Mrs. Smith, along with her cousins from New Mexico, are planning to attend the festivities.".

    a) her cousins from

    b) to attend

    c) are

957. Choose the wrong word: "Geochemistry includes the study of the movement of elements from one place to another as a result of processes chemical.".

    a) processes chemical

    b) the study of

    c) as a

958. Choose the wrong word: "Spell correctly is easy with the aid of a number of word processing programs for personal computers.".

    a) correctly

    b) Spell

    c) computers

959. Choose the wrong word: "Esperanto is an unique language because it was created by a man called Zamenhoff.".

    a) was created

    b) a

    c) an unique

960. Choose the wrong word: "Every student must make up their own study list of the classes he is going to take at the beginning of the quarter.".

    a) their own

    b) he is

    c) the quarter

961. Choose the wrong word: "We had planned to go to the movies but because of the amount of work I had I spend the evening to study.".

    a) had

    b) to the movies

    c) to study

962. Choose the wrong word: "Because the residents had worked so diligent to renovate the old building, the director had a party.".

    a) Because

    b) diligent

    c) renovate

963. Choose the wrong word: "A space is the last frontier for man to conquer.".

    a) A space

    b) is

    c) to conquer

964. Choose the wrong word: "Magnesium, the lightest of our structural metals, has an important place among common engineering materials because of their weight.".

    a) because of

    b) among

    c) their

965. Choose the wrong word: "Fountain pens first became commercial available about a hundred years ago.".

    a) first

    b) commercial

    c) ago

966. Choose the wrong word: "In this novel, Hemmingway tried to capture the feelings the American people at the end of World War I.".

    a) feelings the

    b) to capture

    c) the end of

967. Choose the wrong word: "Upon reading this book by Mark Twain, one begins to understand the value of your common sense.".

    a) by

b) of your

c) to understand

968. Choose the wrong word: "It's essential that cancer is diagnosed and treated as early as possible.".

    a) is diagnosed

    b) as early as

    c) essential

969. Choose the wrong word: "The system for helping slaves escape to the north was called the Underground Railroad, though it was neither underground or a railroad.".

    a) for helping

    b) it

    c) or

970. Choose the wrong word: "Labor Day is always celebrated on first Monday in September.".

    a) first

    b) celebrated

    c) September

971. Choose the wrong word: "The regulation requires that everyone who holds a non-immigrant visa reports his address to the federal government in January of each year.".

    a) holds

    b) reports

    c) who

972. Choose the wrong word: "Bronze after being heated by a strong flame will change color, especially when exposure to hydrogen.".

    a) after being

    b) will

    c) exposure

973. Choose the wrong word: "Daniel is not enough intelligent to pass this economics class without help.".

    a) enough intelligent

    b) this

    c) to pass

974. Choose the wrong word: "If dinosaurs would have continued roaming the earth, man would have evolved quite differently.".
> a) roaming
> b) would have
> c) man

975. Choose the wrong word: "The vase has the same design, but it is different shaped from that one.".
> a) the same
> b) shaped
> c) different

976. Choose the wrong word: "Mercury and alcohol are widely used in thermometers because their volume increases uniform with temperature.".
> a) widely
> b) uniform with
> c) their volume

977. Choose the wrong word: "At the awards banquet, the philanthropist was recognized for his generosity and careful in aiding the poor.".
> a) careful
> b) was recognized
> c) aiding

978. Choose the wrong word: "A catalytic agent such as platinum may be used so the chemical reaction advances more rapidly.".
> a) such as
> b) so
> c) rapidly

979. Choose the wrong word: "It has been proven that when a subject identifies a substance as tasting well, he is often associating the taste with the smell.".
> a) he
> b) associating
> c) well

980. Choose the wrong word: "Plant cuttings who are placed in water will develop roots and can then be planted in soil.".
> a) who

b) placed

c) then be

981. Choose the wrong word: "Neither the mathematics department nor the biology department at the university requires that the students must write a thesis in order to graduate with a master's degree.".

a) nor

b) to graduate

c) must write

982. Choose the wrong word: "In 1985 the world population rose to over 4.7 billion, up almost 85 million from an estimate made the year ago.".

a) rose to

b) ago

c) estimate

983. Choose the wrong word: "It took the mayor over an hour explanation to the other members of the board why he had missed the last meeting.".

a) explanation

b) over an

c) of

984. Choose the wrong word: "The rest of the stockholders will receive his reports in the mail along with a copy of today's proceedings.".

a) will receive

b) in the mail

c) his

985. Choose the wrong word: "The human ear cannot hear a sound that vibrates less than 16 times the second.".

a) cannot

b) the

c) less than

986. Choose the wrong word: "In Canada, the flowing of the maple sap is one of the first sign of spring.".

a) In

b) the flowing

c) sign

987. Choose the wrong word: "Our new neighbors had been living in Arizona since ten years before moving to their present house.".

a) since

b) Our new

c) before moving

988. Choose the wrong word: "They said that the man jumped of the bridge and plunged into the freezing water.".

a) jumped

b) of

c) plunged into

989. Choose the wrong word: "My brother is who wrote the spy story upon which the movie we saw was based.".

a) wrote

b) upon

c) is

990. Choose the wrong word: "The congressman, accompanied by secret service agents an aides, are preparing to enter the convention hall within the next few minutes.".

a) to enter

b) are

c) by

991. Choose the wrong word: "One kinds of tool that was popular during the Stone Age was a flake, used for cutting and scraping.".

a) was

b) for cutting

c) kinds of tool

992. Choose the wrong word: "Today was such beautiful day that I couldn't bring myself to complete all my chores.".

a) such beautiful day

b) myself

c) to complete

993. Choose the wrong word: "The decision to withdraw all support from the activities of the athletes are causing an uproar among the athlete's fans.".

a) all support

b) are causing

c) among

994. Choose the wrong word: "Almost one-half of those taking specialized course's last year were taking self-improvement course.".
    a) course's
    b) Almost
    c) specialized

995. Choose the wrong word: "Many of the population in the rural areas is composed of manual laborers.".
    a) rural areas
    b) Many
    c) composed of

996. Choose the wrong word: "Alcoholic beverages vary widely in content, ranging from only 2 or 3 percent for some light beers to as high to 60 percent for some vodkas and brandies.".
    a) as high to
    b) widely
    c) from

997. Choose the wrong word: "It is necessary that one met a judge before signing the final papers for a divorce.".
    a) before signing
    b) for a divorce
    c) met

998. Choose the wrong word: "Their asked us, David and I, whether we thought that the statistics had been presented fairly and accurately.".
    a) thought
    b) Their
    c) fairly

999. Choose the wrong word: "When a child, she played the guitar, banjo and saxophone in her family's band.".
    a) When
    b) played
    c) band

1000. Choose the wrong word: "When a patient's blood pressure is much higher than it should be, a doctor usually insists that he will not smoke.".
    a) than it

b) should be
c) will not

1001. Choose the wrong word: "Mr. Smith used to jogging in the crisp morning air during the winter months, but now he has stopped.".
    a) crisp morning
    b) during
    c) jogging

1002. Choose the wrong word: "Frank has been acclaimed by colleagues as the greater of all modern architects.".
    a) the greater
    b) by colleagues
    c) as

1003. Choose the wrong word: "The Wagner Act guarantees workers in the U.S. the right to organizing labor unions.".
    a) workers
    b) organizing
    c) the right

1004. Choose the wrong word: "People entering a tropical jungle for the first time are always amazed at how wet it is, how green it is and its incredible beauty.".
    a) entering
    b) for the first time
    c) its incredible beauty

1005. Choose the wrong word: "It was Mr. Bering. the Danish sea captain, who discovered Alaska on its voyage to Russia in 1741.".
    a) its
    b) who
    c) to Russia

1006. Choose the wrong word: "The word "classic" comes of Latin and initially meant "superior".".
    a) comes of
    b) initially
    c) meant

1007. Choose the wrong word: "One of the most popular major field of study for foreign scholars in the US is business and the another is engineering.".

    a) foreign scholars

    b) is

    c) the another

1008. Choose the wrong word: "As soon as the company has as enough earnings to make up for a bad year, the stockholders of cumulative preferred stock receive dividends for the bad year as well as for the good year.".

    a) as enough earnings

    b) to make up for

    c) as well

1009. Choose the wrong word: "Until recently, photocopy machines were regarded strict as business and professional office equipment that required a lot of expensive servicing.".

    a) were regarded

    b) strict as

    c) that required

1010. Choose the wrong word: "The oxygen content of Mars is not sufficient enough to support life as we know it.".

    a) to support

    b) sufficient enough

    c) as

1011. Choose the wrong word: "Studies show that the new strategy is not so effective as the previous one.".

    a) Studies

    b) so

    c) that the

1012. Choose the wrong word: "It's generally accepted that the common cold is caused by as much as forty strains of viruses that may be present in the air.".

    a) as much as

b) is caused

c) by

1013. Choose the wrong word: "Mr. Longfellow was not only a poet and an author but also presided the modern language department at Harvard University for more than ten years.".

    a) also

    b) more than

    c) presided

1014. Choose the wrong word: "Mirrors done of shiny metal were used by the Egyptians in ancient times.".

    a) were used

    b) done

    c) times

1015. Choose the wrong word: "This state, is known for its mild winters, has become the new home for many senior citizens.".

    a) is known

    b) senior

    c) its

1016. Choose the wrong word: "Doctors believe there is better in this modern world of ours to try to prevent illnesses than to rely on medicines to cure them.".

    a) of ours

    b) Doctors

    c) there is

1017. Choose the wrong word: "Sarah and her sister just bought two new winters coats at the clearance sale.".

    a) two new

    b) winters

    c) her sister

1018. Choose the wrong word: "Twenty the amino acids serve as building blocks of proteins.".

    a) Twenty the

    b) serve

    c) blocks

1019. Choose the wrong word: "The Rhode Island is the smallest state in the US.".
   a) The
   b) smallest
   c) the US

1020. Choose the wrong word: "The fire began in the fifth floor of the hotel, but it soon spread to adjacent floors.".
   a) fifth
   b) soon spread
   c) in

1021. Choose the wrong word: "Dresses, skirts, shoes and children's clothing are advertised at great reduced prices this weekend.".
   a) are advertised
   b) great
   c) clothing

1022. Choose the wrong word: "Quasars, which relatively small objects, emit an enormous amount of energy.".
   a) which
   b) emit
   c) amount

1023. Choose the wrong word: "They designed the two-hundred-inch telescope on Mount Palomar study the structure of the universe.".
   a) on Mount Palomar
   b) study
   c) two-hundred-inch

1024. Choose the wrong word: "Mr. Hoover has served as director of the FBI from 1924 until 1972.".
   a) has served
   b) as director
   c) the FBI

1025. Choose the wrong word: "The officials object to them wearing long dresses for the inaugural dance at the country club.".
   a) wearing

b) at the country club

c) them

1026. Choose the wrong word: "Walter Hunt, although was not credited for many of his inventions, is known for the invention of safety-pin.".

    a) credited for

    b) the invention

    c) although was

1027. Choose the wrong word: "There is fewer rainfall on the West Coast of the US than on the East Coast.".

    a) fewer

    b) rainfall

    c) on the

1028. Choose the wrong word: "Neither of the girls have turned in the term papers to the instructor yet.".

    a) the girls

    b) have

    c) to the

1029. Choose the wrong word: "The larger of the forty-eight continental states in the US is Texas.".

    a) continental

    b) in the

    c) larger

1030. Choose the wrong word: "Bats use echoes of their own high-frequency sounds to detect food and avoiding obstacles.".

    a) avoiding obstacles

    b) their own

    c) high-frequency

1031. Choose the wrong word: "By the mid-nineteenth century land was such expensive in large cities that architects began to conserve space by designing skyscrapers.".

    a) conserve

    b) by designing

    c) such expensive

1032. Choose the wrong word: "We decided together with other members of the Astronomy Club to stay up all night to work the full noon next.".
 a) together with
 b) next
 c) other

1033. Choose the wrong word: "The Department of Foreign Languages are not located in the new building opposite the old one.".
 a) opposite
 b) are
 c) in

1034. Choose the wrong word: "Among the world's 44 richest countries, there has been not war since 1945.".
 a) Among the
 b) there
 c) not

1035. Choose the wrong word: "Some researchers believe that an unfair attitude toward the poor will contributed to the problem of poverty.".
 a) contributed
 b) Some researchers
 c) poor

1036. Choose the wrong word: "Nowadays illegally documents purchased are much more difficult to recognize than before.".
 a) much more
 b) than before
 c) illegally documents purchased

1037. Choose the wrong word: "Because there are less members present tonight than there were last night, we must wait until the next meeting to vote.".
 a) than
 b) less
 c) to vote

1038. Choose the wrong word: "The ordinary cold, which is ours most common sickness, is a rival disease whose cure has not yet been found.".
 a) ours

b) which is

c) cure

1039. Choose the wrong word: "After studying all the new materials, the student was able to rise his test score.".

    a) After studying

    b) rise

    c) was able

1040. Choose the wrong word: "Under the crust of the Earth are bubbling hot liquids that sometime rise to the surface.".

    a) bubbling

    b) liquids

    c) sometime

1041. Choose the wrong word: "So good the salesman was that he passed his target after only six months in the job.".

    a) he

    b) in

    c) was

1042. Choose the wrong word: "Mathematics is such important field and serves so many of the sciences that it is a prerequisite for studying every scientific discipline.".

    a) such important

    b) is

    c) for studying

1043. Choose the wrong word: "Before lumberjacks had mechanical equipments, they used horses and ropes to drag logs.".

    a) Before

    b) equipments

    c) drag

1044. Choose the wrong word: "This frog should be avoided because their skin secretions are lethal to small animals and irritating to humans.".

    a) their

    b) should be avoided

    c) irritating

1045. Choose the wrong word: "Grandma Smith having been able to continue farming, she might never have begun to paint.".
>   a) paint
>   b) farming
>   c) having

1046. Choose the wrong word: "Grasses form a substantial partly of the diet of many ruminants.".
>   a) form
>   b) partly
>   c) substantial

1047. Choose the wrong word: "The students were tired when they finally arrived at the ruins had read about he previous right.".
>   a) had read
>   b) were
>   c) finally

1048. Choose the wrong word: "When there is a few money remaining after all expenses have been paid, we say that a small economic surplus has been created.".
>   a) there is
>   b) a few
>   c) have been paid

1049. Choose the wrong word: "My brother is in Spain on vacation, but I wish he was here so that he could help me repair my car.".
>   a) in
>   b) on
>   c) was

1050. Choose the wrong word: "Almost poetry is more enjoyable when it is read aloud.".
>   a) is more
>   b) Almost
>   c) it is

1051. Choose the wrong word: "A number of novels submitted their manuscripts under pseudonyms to conceal the fact that they were women.".

a) novels

b) to conceal

c) they were

1052. Choose the wrong word: "In the ionosphere gases have been partly ionized for high frequency radiation from the sun and other sources.".

a) partly

b) other sources

c) for high frequency

1053. Choose the wrong word: "Dislike the gorilla, the male adult chimpanzee weighs under 200 pounds.".

a) Dislike

b) male

c) under

1054. Choose the wrong word: "Each of the students in the accounting class has to type their own research paper this semester.".

a) students

b) their

c) own

1055. Choose the wrong word: "The flag of the original first colonies may or may not have been made by Mrs. Ross during the Revolution.".

a) original first

b) have been made

c) during the Revolution

1056. Choose the wrong word: "For the first time in the history of the country, the person which was recommended by the president to replace a retiring justice on the Supreme Court is a woman.".

a) retiring

b) which

c) to replace

1057. Choose the wrong word: "The high protein content of alfalfa plants, along with the characteristically long root system, make them particularly valuable in arid countries.".

a) particularly

b) valuable

c) make

1058. Choose the wrong word: "Psychological experiment indicate that people remember more math problems that they cannot solve than those they are able to solve.".

    a) solve

    b) experiment

    c) those

1059. Choose the wrong word: "Aristotle systematically set out the various forms of the syllogism that has remained an important reference for logic.".

    a) various

    b) has remained

    c) that

1060. Choose the wrong word: "While the sun is the major source of ultraviolet rays, it is not the source only.".

    a) source only

    b) the major

    c) While

1061. Choose the wrong word: "Lead poisoning can result if to much lead builds up in the body.".

    a) to

    b) builds up

    c) poisoning

1062. Choose the wrong word: "Every society changes, but not change at the same rate or in the same direction.".

    a) same rate

    b) Every society

    c) but not change

1063. Choose the wrong word: "Natural gas often occurs both together with petroleum in the minute pores of rocks such as sandstone and limestone.".

    a) occurs

b) both together

c) such as

1064. Choose the wrong word: "The NBA will not let any athlete to continue playing in the league unless he submits voluntarily to treatment for drug addiction.".

    a) to continue

    b) playing

    c) drug addiction

1065. Choose the wrong word: "Water insects have multitudes of little branching tubes within them bodies which are always full of air.".

    a) have

    b) them

    c) which

1066. Choose the wrong word: "Sarah is finally used to cook on an electric stove after having a gas one for so long.".

    a) after having

    b) for so long

    c) cook

1067. Choose the wrong word: "Lack of sanitation in restaurants are a major cause of disease in some areas of the country.".

    a) sanitation

    b) are

    c) cause

1068. Choose the wrong word: "The primary concern of a central bank is to maintenance of a sound based commercial banking structure.".

    a) concern

    b) sound based

    c) to maintenance

1069. Choose the wrong word: "Before she moved to Boston, with its much milder climate, Sarah found that her health improved considerably.".

    a) Before

    b) with

    c) found that

1070. Choose the wrong word: "From the airplane passengers are able to clearly see the outline of the whole island.".
  a) able
  b) to clearly see
  c) of

1071. Choose the wrong word: "After she invented the cotton gin in 1793, the cotton market had boomed.".
  a) had boomed
  b) the
  c) in 1793

1072. Choose the wrong word: "Natural gas is compose of hydrocarbon molecules that break apart into hydrogen and carbon atoms when heated.".
  a) that break
  b) apart into
  c) compose

1073. Choose the wrong word: "Wind is the motion that occurs when lighter air rises and cools heavier air replaces it.".
  a) that occurs
  b) cools
  c) lighter

1074. Choose the wrong word: "Had the committee members considered the alternatives more carefully, they would have realized that the second was better as the first.".
  a) as the first
  b) more carefully
  c) second was

1075. Choose the wrong word: "Although a doctor may be able to diagnose a problem perfect, he still may not be able to find a drug to which the patient will respond.".
  a) to diagnose
  b) perfect
  c) be able to

1076. Choose the wrong word: "The report is released by the Commodity Futures Trading Commission on eleven day of each month.".

    a) released by

    b) on eleven

    c) month

1077. Choose the wrong word: "All data in computer are changed into electronic pulses by an input unit.".

    a) into

    b) unit

    c) in computer

1078. Choose the wrong word: "The lion has long been a symbol of strength, power and it is very cruel.".

    a) it is very cruel

    b) long

    c) the

1079. Choose the wrong word: "She won the Pulitzer Prize in American history for her biographer of Paul Revere.".

    a) won

    b) biographer

    c) in

1080. Choose the wrong word: "To see the Statue of Liberty and taking pictures from the top of the Empire State Building are two reasons for visiting New York City.".

    a) from

    b) for visiting

    c) taking

1081. Choose the wrong word: "It is imperative that a graduate student maintains a grade point average of B in his major field.".

    a) maintains

    b) of

    c) It is

1082. Choose the wrong word: "The fossils represent animals or plants that had hard and usually well-developed body structure.".

    a) that had

b) hard

c) The fossils

1083. Choose the wrong word: "Air pollution, together with littering, are causing many problems in our large, industrial cities today.".

    a) are

    b) many

    c) with

1084. Choose the wrong word: "The woman had took the money from the cash register before she left for lunch.".

    a) The

    b) had took

    c) she left

1085. Choose the wrong word: "When her novel appeared in 1922, critics were divided as to how good it was written.".

    a) as to

    b) good

    c) written

1086. Choose the wrong word: "The practical and legal implications of euthanasia, the practice of causing the death of a person suffering from an incurable disease, are so controversial as it is illegal in most countries.".

    a) suffering

    b) in most countries

    c) as

1087. Choose the wrong word: "The federal government recommends that all expectant women will not only refrain from smoking but also avoid places where other people smoke.".

    a) will not only refrain

    b) smoke

    c) recommends that

1088. Choose the wrong word: "Above 80 percent of the laborers at the construction site are temporary workers.".

    a) laborers

    b) Above

    c) site

1089. Choose the wrong word: "Either a savings and loan company or a bank can borrow money to those people who want to buy a home.".

    a) or

    b) to buy

    c) borrow

1090. Choose the wrong word: "Because of the long drought citizens were told that it was imperative that in future they will save as much water as possible.".

    a) will

    b) citizens

    c) much

1091. Choose the wrong word: "The color of the Red Sea is due to a minute alga or sea plant, whose forms huge patches of a blood red tint.".

    a) a minute alga

    b) sea plant

    c) whose

1092. Choose the wrong word: "The church it was open, and the choir was having a last minute rehearsal.".

    a) open

    b) was having

    c) it

1093. Choose the wrong word: "The prime rate is the rate of interest that a bank will charge when it borrows money to its best clients.".

    a) borrows

    b) it

    c) its

1094. Choose the wrong word: "In 1903, when they announced they had invented a flying machine, his news was generally ignored.".

    a) when

    b) his

    c) generally

1095. Choose the wrong word: "In today's competitive markets, even small businesses had better to advertise on TV and radio in order to gain a share of the market.".

a) today's

b) to gain

c) to advertise

1096. Choose the wrong word: "At present, I am a student at the Technical College, which I am studying English part-time.".

    a) which

    b) am studying

    c) at

1097. Choose the wrong word: "One of the girl who worked in that company died.".

    a) who

    b) the girl

    c) worked

1098. Choose the wrong word: "This lesson is such long that I have written it for 30 minutes.".

    a) such

    b) that

    c) have written

1099. Choose the wrong word: "When Mr. Smith woke up he found himself in a country what very small people lived.".

    a) woke up

    b) lived

    c) what

1100. Choose the wrong word: "It is believed that the wanted man was living in London.".

    a) was living

    b) wanted

    c) in

1101. Choose the wrong word: "The letter was typed clear and careful, but without any address or signature.".

    a) was typed

    b) clear and careful

    c) without

1102. Choose the wrong word: "The blind is unable to see anything.".

    a) anything

    b) is

    c) to see

1103. Choose the wrong word: "How far English do you know? asked my friend.".

    a) How far

    b) do

    c) asked

1104. Choose the wrong word: "I will come back as quickly as possible.".

    a) will come

    b) possible

    c) quickly

1105. Choose the wrong word: "A large number of students in this school speaks French fairly fluently.".

    a) A large number of

    b) students

    c) speaks

1106. Choose the wrong word: "Did she use to be your next-door neighbor? Yes, but I never did liked her.".

    a) use to be

    b) liked

    c) Did

1107. Choose the wrong word: "All the youth must contribute to building of the country.".

    a) building of

    b) to

    c) must contribute

1108. Choose the wrong word: "We can prevent flood by preservation the forests.".

    a) can prevent

    b) the forests

    c) preservation

1109. Choose the wrong word: "Does the grass need be cut?".
   a) need
   b) be cut
   c) Does

1110. Choose the wrong word: "Jane said she is 18 years the following week.".
   a) is
   b) said
   c) years

1111. Choose the wrong word: "Are you saying you would ever see her again?".
   a) saying
   b) again
   c) would ever see

1112. Choose the wrong word: "Each of you have a share in the work.".
   a) a share
   b) have
   c) Each of

1113. Choose the wrong word: "He said that he was doing his homework since 7 o'clock.".
   a) was doing
   b) said
   c) since

1114. Choose the wrong word: "What had you been doing during the last few weeks?".
   a) been doing
   b) during
   c) had

1115. Choose the wrong word: "How many times have you seen them so far? A few time.".
   a) time
   b) so far
   c) How many

1116. Choose the wrong word: "Had your brother enjoyed the party last night? I think so. He always enjoys your parties.".
    a) think
    b) enjoys
    c) Had you brother enjoyed

1117. Choose the wrong word: "I have been waiting for my brother. I wonder if he had lost his way.".
    a) wonder
    b) had lost
    c) for

1118. Choose the wrong word: "The doctors know that it will be difficult to save the life of this patient, but they did their best.".
    a) know
    b) will be
    c) did

1119. Choose the wrong word: "He said that everything will be all right.".
    a) will be
    b) everything
    c) all right

1120. Choose the wrong word: "They said that the custom has dated back to the feudal period.".
    a) said
    b) back
    c) has dated

1121. Choose the wrong word: "He had been teaching since twenty-five years before he retired last year.".
    a) before
    b) retired
    c) since

1122. Choose the wrong word: "In a few hours, we have finished the test, and we'll go home and rest.".
    a) the test
    b) have finished
    c) a few

1123. Choose the wrong word: "What will you do when you leave for school?".

    a) for
    b) will you do
    c) when

1124. Choose the wrong word: "The result was quite different with what I expected.".

    a) was
    b) different
    c) with

1125. Choose the wrong word: "What seems easy for you seems difficult to me.".

    a) for
    b) seems easy
    c) to

1126. Choose the wrong word: "Your personality is important for the success of your work.".

    a) personality
    b) for
    c) of

1127. Choose the wrong word: "The surgeon is a genius. We are not doubtful on it.".

    a) is
    b) on
    c) genius

1128. Choose the wrong word: "Why are you angry with me? I hadn't do anything wrong.".

    a) are
    b) with
    c) hadn't do

1129. Choose the wrong word: "We have to start early because we won't be late.".

    a) because

b) have to

c) early

1130. Choose the wrong word: "Don't let a good chance going by.".
    a) Don't let
    b) going
    c) a

1131. Choose the wrong word: "Being good for agricultural purposes, soil must have in it the minerals plants require.".
    a) must have
    b) require
    c) Being good

1132. Choose the wrong word: "He had to explain the lesson very clear so that his students could understand it.".
    a) clear
    b) had to
    c) so that

1133. Choose the wrong word: "Doctors are using laser beam to remove of bone in ear surgery.".
    a) are using
    b) of
    c) to remove

1134. Choose the wrong word: "We wish today was sunny so that we could spend the day in the country communing with nature.".
    a) so that
    b) was
    c) could spend

1135. Choose the wrong word: "Before I moved to another place, the man who lives across the street often helped me with my English.".
    a) moved
    b) often helped
    c) lives

1136. Choose the wrong word: "Upon hatching, young ducks known how to swim.".

a) Upon

b) known

c) hatching

1137. Choose the wrong word: "In order of go abroad, one must present a medical report.".

    a) In order of

    b) a

    c) medical

1138. Choose the wrong word: "In many ways, riding a bicycle is similar to when driving a car.".

    a) riding

    b) similar to

    c) when

1139. Choose the wrong word: "The speaker is very well-acquainted of the subject.".

    a) of

    b) very

    c) well-acquainted

1140. Choose the wrong word: "If you burn the garbage, it will give off unpleased odor.".

    a) will give

    b) unpleased

    c) burn

1141. Choose the wrong word: "They have different cultures; that was why they often have different ways of living.".

    a) cultures

    b) have

    c) that was why

1142. Choose the wrong word: "You have to study hardly to keep pace with your classmates.".

    a) hardly

    b) have to

    c) study

1143. Choose the wrong word: "After you graduate from the university, you still have to go on study.".
  a) graduate
  b) study
  c) have to

1144. Choose the wrong word: "A free educating is guaranteed to every citizen.".
  a) every
  b) educating
  c) A

1145. Choose the wrong word: "Whenever students asked for help or guidance, the counselor would advise them or refer them to someone who will.".
  a) will
  b) for help
  c) would advise

1146. Choose the wrong word: "Her coat was laying on the floor.".
  a) Her coat
  b) was
  c) laying

1147. Choose the wrong word: "It took her for a long time to throw off her bad cold because of her poor health.".
  a) took
  b) for
  c) because of

1148. Choose the wrong word: "There is nothing better than take a boat on the lake in the park in the afternoon.".
  a) There is
  b) take
  c) better than

1149. Choose the wrong word: "I lost my temper of the customs official.".
  a) of
  b) temper
  c) official

1150. Choose the wrong word: "The twins look so alike their grandmother.".

    a) The twins

    b) look

    c) alike

1151. Choose the wrong word: "Sarah's appearance at the reception with that man cause something of a rumor.".

    a) appearance

    b) cause

    c) at the reception

1152. Choose the wrong word: "It is difficult to get used to sleep in a tent after having a soft, comfortable bed to lie on.".

    a) to sleep

    b) difficult

    c) bed to lie on

1153. Choose the wrong word: "They used to spending their summer holidays at the seaside when they were children.".

    a) used to

    b) were

    c) spending

1154. Choose the wrong word: "David has got extreme bushy eyebrows.".

    a) has got

    b) extreme

    c) bushy

1155. Choose the wrong word: "A confidence woman is needed to look after two naughty children.".

    a) is needed

    b) to look after

    c) confidence

1156. Choose the wrong word: "Mary pretended not having been hurt when her younger brother bit her.".

    a) having been

    b) hurt

    c) bit

1157. Choose the wrong word: "How beautiful the painting was! I stood there being admired it for a long time.".

  a) stood
  b) How beautiful
  c) being admired

1158. Choose the wrong word: "I'm sure it's not my fault that Dave found out what we were planning. I don't remember being told anyone about it.".

  a) being told
  b) sure
  c) about

1159. Choose the wrong word: "Could you locate the person which wallet you found?".

  a) Could
  b) which
  c) found

1160. Choose the wrong word: "I made the soup by mixing a few meat with some rice.".

  a) made
  b) a few
  c) some

1161. Choose the wrong word: "A good teacher makes her students to view the world from new perspectives.".

  a) to view
  b) makes
  c) from

1162. Choose the wrong word: "Do you think English is an important language for master?".

  a) Do you think
  b) is
  c) for master

1163. Choose the wrong word: "Have you ever been to Madrid? Yes, I have been there much times.".

  a) ever been to

b) much

c) have been

1164. Choose the wrong word: "Be patient. Don't expect to learn a foreign language for a week.".

    a) for a week

    b) patient

    c) to learn

1165. Choose the wrong word: "A good knowledge of English will help you finding a job more easily.".

    a) will help

    b) more easily

    c) finding

1166. Choose the wrong word: "Many countries have past laws restricting hunting and fishing to protect the resources.".

    a) have past

    b) restricting

    c) to protect

1167. Choose the wrong word: "Smoke of factories will pollute the air.".

    a) of

    b) will pollute

    c) air

1168. Choose the wrong word: "Burning coal and oil will release gases harmful to human.".

    a) will release

    b) human

    c) harmful to

1169. Choose the wrong word: "Why don't you discard this broken old bicycle? It is useless now.".

    a) is

    b) broken old

    c) useless

1170. Choose the wrong word: "A girl may or may not shake hands when she is introduced with a man.".

a) with

b) shake hands

c) is introduced

1171. Choose the wrong word: "I won't permit nobody to make a mess in my house.".

    a) nobody

    b) to make

    c) in

1172. Choose the wrong word: "He denied that he has been involved in the decision not to attack the enemy position.".

    a) in

    b) denied that

    c) has been involved

1173. Choose the wrong word: "She said that she was supposed being in Germany this weekend.".

    a) said

    b) being

    c) in

1174. Choose the wrong word: "Sarah said that she would like to be in one of that teacher's class.".

    a) to be

    b) teacher's class

    c) would like

1175. Choose the wrong word: "My cousin is studying English. She started to learn it two years ago. She had studied English for two years.".

    a) had studied

    b) for two years

    c) is studying

1176. Choose the wrong word: "She is worried with failing her final exam in physics.".

    a) is worried

    b) final

    c) with failing

1177. Choose the wrong word: "I wish I listened to him. Now it is too late.".

      a) wish

      b) to

      c) listened

1178. Choose the wrong word: "American woman are used to being independent.".

      a) woman

      b) are used to being

      c) woman

1179. Choose the wrong word: "We don't approve of your behave that way.".

      a) don't approve

      b) behave

      c) your

1180. Choose the wrong word: "One of history's most spectacular executions were that of Damien's.".

      a) One of

      b) spectacular

      c) were

1181. Choose the wrong word: "Studying the science of logic is one way to cultivate one's reason skills.".

      a) reason

      b) science of

      c) way to

1182. Choose the wrong word: "A farmer's tractor is like a powerful horse, as it plows field, pulls trailers and moves heavy loads.".

      a) is like

      b) field

      c) moves

1183. Choose the wrong word: "Mr. Burbank earned the funds to go west by sale his new ideas about growing potatoes.".

      a) the funds

b) about

c) sale

1184. Choose the wrong word: "When the second World War, almost a third of a million people were killed.".

    a) of

    b) almost

    c) When

1185. Choose the wrong word: "They will check my blood eight weeks from now to see how good I'm responding to the treatment.".

    a) how good

    b) from now

    c) will check

1186. Choose the wrong word: "Cotton used to rank first between crops, but it represents only a fraction of the agricultural production now.".

    a) rank

    b) between

    c) represents only

1187. Choose the wrong word: "Salmon lay their eggs and die in fresh water, although they live in salt water when most of their adult lives.".

    a) when

    b) lay

    c) adult lives

1188. Choose the wrong word: "To building their nests, tailorbirds use their bills as needles.".

    a) nests

    b) building

    c) their

1189. Choose the wrong word: "Drugs are one of the medicine profession's most valuable tools.".

    a) are

    b) tools

    c) medicine

1190. Choose the wrong word: "With its strong claws and its many protruding tooth a gopher is an excellent digger.".
    a) protruding tooth
    b) strong claws
    c) With

1191. Choose the wrong word: "Drug addiction has resulted of many destroyed careers, and expulsions from school or college.".
    a) has
    b) destroyed
    c) of

1192. Choose the wrong word: "Because of that expedition, the US begin to realize the true value of this territory.".
    a) begin
    b) territory
    c) Because

1193. Choose the wrong word: "Americans annually import more than 3 billion dollars' worthy of Italian clothing, jewelry and shoes.".
    a) clothing
    b) worthy
    c) more

1194. Choose the wrong word: "Mrs. Smith, she spent her life working with the health and welfare of the families of workers.".
    a) she
    b) her life
    c) welfare

1195. Choose the wrong word: "There are many different ways of comparing the economy of one nation with those of another.".
    a) another
    b) There are
    c) those

1196. Choose the wrong word: "Male guppies, like many other male fish, are more color than females.".
    a) color

b) Male

c) like

1197. Choose the wrong word: "When rhinos take mud baths, the mud create a barrier to biting insects.".

    a) the

    b) create

    c) biting

1198. Choose the wrong word: "Benjamin Franklin, as an inventor, he had broad interests, mechanical skills, persistence, and a practical view of life.".

    a) he

    b) as an

    c) of

1199. Choose the wrong word: "In the stock market, the fluctuations in Standard and Poor's 500 Index does not always conform to Dow Jones Averages.".

    a) always

    b) In

    c) does

1200. Choose the wrong word: "A jellyfish, which isn't really a fish, it has no brain, no bones and no face.".

    a) it

    b) isn't

    c) bones

1201. Choose the wrong word: "International trade, going travelling and television have lain the groundwork for modern global life styles.".

    a) have lain

    b) going travelling

    c) for

1202. Choose the wrong word: "The most visible remind of the close relationship between the US and France is the famous Statue of Liberty, which stands in New York harbour.".

    a) between

b) is

c) remind

1203. Choose the wrong word: "Until diamonds are cut and polished, they like look small blue-grey stones.".
   a) like look
   b) Until
   c) stones

1204. Choose the wrong word: "Mr. Robinson, whose joined the team in 1957, was the first black American to play baseball in a major league.".
   a) to play
   b) whose
   c) the

1205. Choose the wrong word: "Laser technology is the heart of a new generation of high-speed copiers and printer.".
   a) is
   b) generation
   c) printer

1206. Choose the wrong word: "Fertilize farmland is one of the biggest natural resources in the Central States.".
   a) Fertilize
   b) one
   c) biggest

1207. Choose the wrong word: "The symptoms of diabetes in the early stages are too slight that people don't notice them.".
   a) the
   b) too
   c) them

1208. Choose the wrong word: "The novel written after Mrs. Mitchell quit her job as a reporter because of an ankle injury.".
   a) quit
   b) as
   c) written

1209. Choose the wrong word: "Air pollution becomes a particular serious problem, however, when smoke soot, fumes and other man-made pollutants are dispersed into the air in large amounts.".

    a) particular

    b) however

    c) are dispersed

1210. Choose the wrong word: "Scientists and engineers have invented filters and other methods of removing pollutants for industrial waste.".

    a) waste

    b) for

    c) have invented

1211. Choose the wrong word: "In order to survive, trees rely to the amount of annual rainfall they receive, as well as the seasonal distribution of the rain.".

    a) as well as

    b) of

    c) rely to

1212. Choose the wrong word: "The purchased this area was one of the biggest events in the history of the family.".

    a) events

    b) purchased

    c) was

1213. Choose the wrong word: "A future system of solid waste management should begin with reduce in the amount of waste.".

    a) reduce

    b) amount of

    c) solid

1214. Choose the wrong word: "The tongue is the principle organ of taste and is crucial for chewing, swallowed and speaking.".

    a) swallowed

    b) of taste

    c) principle

1215. Choose the wrong word: "The members of both companies are election by the employees.".

a) both

b) members

c) election

1216. Choose the wrong word: "The human ear cannot hear a sound that vibrates less than 16 times the second.".

    a) the

    b) that

    c) cannot

1217. Choose the wrong word: "Some tree frogs can alter their colors in order to blending to their environment.".

    a) can alter

    b) blending

    c) in order

1218. Choose the wrong word: "If one is invited out to a dinner, it is perfectly proper to go either with or without no a gift.".

    a) to go

    b) one

    c) no

1219. Choose the wrong word: "Some birds, such as quails, can move instant from a resting position to full flight.".

    a) resting

    b) to

    c) instant

1220. Choose the wrong word: "He launched out in extravagance.".

    a) extravagance

    b) out

    c) in

1221. Choose the wrong word: "Dave's gradually getting over a hear attack, which had kept him off work for nearly two months.".

    a) attack

    b) had kept

    c) over

1222. Choose the wrong word: "The elevator was out of order and I had to walk to tenth floor.".

    a) was

    b) out or order

    c) tenth floor

1223. Choose the wrong word: "She got the job like a model because of her good looks.".

    a) like

    b) looks

    c) got

1224. Choose the wrong word: "You would better cut down on your intake of sugar to avoid problems of your teeth.".

    a) to avoid

    b) of

    c) cut down on

1225. Choose the wrong word: "It was said that the world will be suffering from an energy crisis by the 2030s.".

    a) was said

    b) will be suffering

    c) energy

1226. Choose the wrong word: "Why are you always jealous with other friends?".

    a) are

    b) other

    c) with

1227. Choose the wrong word: "I had tried to get through to Dave for days now. Either he's away or his phone's out of order.".

    a) get through

    b) for days now

    c) I had tried

1228. Choose the wrong word: "Would you buy some banana if the greengrocer's is still open?".

    a) open

b) Would you

c) banana

1229. Choose the wrong word: "There are a lot of multi-storey buildings on the center of Tokyo.".
    a) There are
    b) a lot of
    c) on

1230. Choose the wrong word: "Please go in. She is free for seeing you now.".
    a) for seeing
    b) go in
    c) now

1231. Choose the wrong word: "If you take the car, you would save yourself a lot of times.".
    a) save
    b) times
    c) would

1232. Choose the wrong word: "On behalf of all of us who are here this morning, I would like thanking Mr. Smith for his help.".
    a) all of us
    b) are
    c) thanking

1233. Choose the wrong word: "Today we know that the earth is one of nine planets who orbit the sun.".
    a) who
    b) that
    c) orbit

1234. Choose the wrong word: "James bought this vocabulary book that he could go over all the things he has studied this year.".
    a) has studied
    b) could go over
    c) that

1235. Choose the wrong word: "The two houses stood 600 meters apart from.".

    a) meters
    b) from
    c) stood

1236. Choose the wrong word: "Let's cut through a wood instead for going by the road.".

    a) instead for
    b) going
    c) by

1237. Choose the wrong word: "Unluckily his illness turned out to be extreme infectious.".

    a) Unluckily
    b) extreme
    c) turned out

1238. Choose the wrong word: "The 30% discount in only applicable for items that cost over $500.".

    a) discount
    b) applicable
    c) for

1239. Choose the wrong word: "It was amazed that Smith showed so few grief at his mother's death.".

    a) few
    b) was
    c) amazed

1240. Choose the wrong word: "It's impossible believing that anyone would purposely harm a child, least of all its own mother.".

    a) least of all
    b) believing
    c) impossible

1241. Choose the wrong word: "I find the time of English meals very strange. I'm not accustomed having dinner at 5 pm.".

    a) find

b) strange

c) accustomed having

1242. Choose the wrong word: "She really takes after her father. She had got the same character.".
    a) had
    b) takes after
    c) really

1243. Choose the wrong word: "The market in town was so crowded that she gave in doing her shopping here.".
    a) crowded
    b) in
    c) doing

1244. Choose the wrong word: "Police had better never drinking alcohol on duty.".
    a) drinking
    b) had better
    c) on

1245. Choose the wrong word: "In his opinion, Chinese is a very difficult language to pick out quickly.".
    a) to
    b) difficult
    c) pick out

1246. Choose the wrong word: "Dave has always used to write back as soon as he got my letters, but months can go before I get a rely these days.".
    a) as soon as
    b) get
    c) has always used

1247. Choose the wrong word: "Don't be nervous about sitting for the exam. I know for certain you would pass.".
    a) would pass
    b) sitting for
    c) know

1248. Choose the wrong word: "Tommy seemed to enjoy himself on vacation, hadn't he?".

    a) to enjoy

    b) hadn't he

    c) on

1249. Choose the wrong word: "We have not seen our old teacher in 1990.".

    a) have not seen

    b) in

    c) our

1250. Choose the wrong word: "He has done a valuable contribution to the independence of the country.".

    a) to

    b) valuable

    c) done

1251. Choose the wrong word: "While he watched TV last night, a cat ran across the floor.".

    a) ran

    b) across

    c) watched

1252. Choose the wrong word: "It's high time you should tidy away those toys!".

    a) high time

    b) should tidy

    c) toys

1253. Choose the wrong word: "How about taking some time off? You were working too hard lately. Take a short vacation.".

    a) about

    b) some time off

    c) were working

1254. Choose the wrong word: "Unless his candidate had won the election, he would be happy now.".

    a) Unless

b) would be

c) now

1255. Choose the wrong word: "Her eyes burned and her shoulders ached. She has been sitting at the computer for 6 straight hours. Finally, she took a break.".

    a) ached

    b) has been sitting

    c) took

1256. Choose the wrong word: "The main office of the factory can be found in Oak Street in Boston.".

    a) in

    b) The main

    c) be found

1257. Choose the wrong word: "Because there are less members present tonight than there were last night, we must wait until the next meeting to vote.".

    a) than

    b) to vote

    c) less

1258. Choose the wrong word: "Daniel is particularly fond of cooking, and he often cooks really delicious meals.".

    a) often cooks

    b) really

    c) fond of

1259. Choose the wrong word: "The progress made in space travel for the early 1960s is remarkable.".

    a) in space

    b) for

    c) made

1260. Choose the wrong word: "Sarah has not rarely missed a play or concert since she was seventeen years old.".

    a) not rarely

    b) a play

    c) since

1261. Choose the wrong word: "The governor has not decided how to deal with the new problems already.".

    a) The

    b) already

    c) has

1262. Choose the wrong word: "There was a very interesting news on the radio this morning about the earthquake in Hungary.".

    a) a

    b) There

    c) about

1263. Choose the wrong word: "The professor had already give the homework assignment when he had remembered that Monday was a holiday.".

    a) Monday

    b) had remembered

    c) was

1264. Choose the wrong word: "Having been beaten by the police for striking an officer, the man will cry out in pain.".

    a) for striking

    b) the man

    c) will cry out

1265. Choose the wrong word: "This table is not sturdy enough to support a television, and that one probably isn't neither.".

    a) to support

    b) neither

    c) that one

1266. Choose the wrong word: "The bridge was hitting by a large ship during a sudden storm last week.".

    a) was hitting

    b) during

    c) sudden

1267. Choose the wrong word: "The company representative sold to the manager a sewing machine for forty euros.".

    a) The company

b) to the manager

c) sewing

1268. Choose the wrong word: "The taxi driver told the man to don't allow his disobedient son to hang out the window.".
    a) taxi driver
    b) told the man
    c) to don't allow

1269. Choose the wrong word: "These televisions are quite popular in Europe, but those ones are not.".
    a) quite
    b) those ones
    c) are

1270. Choose the wrong word: "David seldom pays his bills on time ,and his brother does too.".
    a) on time
    b) pays his bills
    c) does too

1271. Choose the wrong word: "The price of crude oil used to be a great deal lower than now, wasn't it?".
    a) lower
    b) great
    c) wasn't it

1272. Choose the wrong word: "When an university formulates new regulations, it must rely its decision to the students and faculty.".
    a) an
    b) it
    c) new regulations

1273. Choose the wrong word: "Daniel was upset last night because he had to do too many homeworks.".
    a) because
    b) upset
    c) many homeworks

1274. Choose the wrong word: "There is some scissors in the desk drawer in the bedroom if you need them.".

    a) scissors

    b) is

    c) in

1275. Choose the wrong word: "The Board of Realtors doesn't have any informations about the increase in rent for this area.".

    a) about

    b) informations

    c) in rent for

1276. Choose the wrong word: "Daniel is not enough intelligent to pass this economics class without your help.".

    a) enough intelligent

    b) to pass

    c) this

1277. Choose the wrong word: "There were so much people trying to leave the burning building that the police had a great deal of trouble controlling them.".

    a) There were

    b) the burning

    c) much

1278. Choose the wrong word: "Mr. Smith lived in New York since 1970 to 1985, but he is now living in Madrid.".

    a) is now living

    b) since

    c) in

1279. Choose the wrong word: "The fire began in the fifth floor of the hotel, but it soon spread to adjacent floors.".

    a) fifth

    b) soon spread

    c) in

1280. Choose the wrong word: "Mrs. Smith was bought a new sports car; however, she has yet to learnt how to drive it.".

    a) learnt

b) has yet

c) was bought

1281. Choose the wrong word: "While searching for the wreckage of a unidentified aircraft, the Coast Guard encountered severe squalls at sea.".

    a) While searching

    b) the

    c) a

1282. Choose the wrong word: "Although a number of police officers was guarding the priceless treasures in the museum, the director worried that someone would try to steal them.".

    a) would try to

    b) steal

    c) was guarding

1283. Choose the wrong word: "Since it was so difficult for Indians to negotiate a peace treaty or declare war in their native language, they used a universal understood form of sign language.".

    a) to negotiate

    b) universal

    c) so difficult

1284. Choose the wrong word: "Mr. Braille designed a form of communication enabling people to convey and preserve their thoughts to incorporate a series of dots which were read by the finger tips.".

    a) enabling

    b) were read

    c) to incorporate

1285. Choose the wrong word: "While verbalization is the most common form of language in existence, humans make use of many others systems and techniques to express their thoughts and feelings.".

    a) existence

    b) to express

    c) others systems

1286. Choose the wrong word: "The need for a well-rounded education was an idea espoused by the Greeks in time of Socrates.".

    a) for

b) in time of

c) espoused

1287. Choose the wrong word: "Writers and media personnel sell theirselves best by the impression given in their verbal expression.".

     a) theirselves

     b) by the

     c) expression

1288. Choose the wrong word: "In the spirit of the naturalist writers, that author's work portrays man's struggle for surviving.".

     a) In the spirit

     b) surviving

     c) author's

1289. Choose the wrong word: "This story is a clinical portrayal of man as an animal trapped by the fear and hunger.".

     a) of man as an animal

     b) a

     c) the fear

1290. Choose the wrong word: "Engineers succeeded on putting more and more components on each silicon chip.".

     a) more and more

     b) on

     c) succeeded

1291. Choose the wrong word: "For a long time, this officials have been known throughout the country as political bosses and law enforcers.".

     a) this

     b) have been known

     c) law enforcers

1292. Choose the wrong word: "Sarah hardly never misses an opportunity to play in the tennis tournaments.".

     a) to play

     b) never

     c) an

1293. Choose the wrong word: "Air pollution, together with littering, are causing many problems in our large, industrial cities today.".

    a) with

    b) in our large

    c) are

1294. Choose the wrong word: "Because of the severe snow storm and the road blocks, the air force dropped food and medical supplies close the city.".

    a) dropped food

    b) close the city

    c) Because of

1295. Choose the wrong word: "Hummingbirds are the only birds capable to fly backward as well as forward, up and down.".

    a) to fly

    b) as well as

    c) forward

1296. Choose the wrong word: "The news of the president's treaty negotiations with the foreign government were received with mixed emotions.".

    a) treaty

    b) were

    c) mixed emotions

1297. Choose the wrong word: "Sarah's bilingual ability and previous experience were the qualities that which helped her get the job over all the other candidates.".

    a) were

    b) the other

    c) that which

1298. Choose the wrong word: "David giving up smoking has caused him to gain weight and become irritable with his acquaintances.".

    a) David

    b) smoking has

    c) become irritable

1299. Choose the wrong word: "They asked me what did happen last night, but I was unable to tell them.".

    a) last night
    b) what did happen
    c) unable to

1300. Choose the wrong word: "The test administrator ordered we not to open our books until he told us to do so.".

    a) not to open
    b) told us
    c) we

1301. Choose the wrong word: "Our new neighbors had been living in this state since ten years before moving to their present house.".

    a) since
    b) Our new
    c) before moving

1302. Choose the wrong word: "I would of attended the meeting of the planning committee last week, but I had to deliver a speech at a convention.".

    a) had to deliver
    b) of the planning
    c) would of

1303. Choose the wrong word: "We are suppose to read all of chapter seven and answer the questions for tomorrow's class.".

    a) all of chapter
    b) answer
    c) suppose

1304. Choose the wrong word: "The explanation that our instructor gave us was different than the one yours gave you.".

    a) our
    b) gave us
    c) than

1305. Choose the wrong word: "In the sixteenth century, this country became involved in foreign wars with several other European countries and could not find the means of finance the battles.".

a) several other

b) of finance

c) became involved

1306. Choose the wrong word: "Neither of the girls have turned in the term papers to the instructor yet.".

    a) girls

    b) have

    c) yet

1307. Choose the wrong word: "After studying all the new materials, the student was able to rise his test score by twenty-five points.".

    a) all the new

    b) was able

    c) rise

1308. Choose the wrong word: "The book that you see laying on the table belongs to the teacher.".

    a) laying

    b) see

    c) belongs to

1309. Choose the wrong word: "I suggest that he goes to the doctor as soon as he returns from taking the exam.".

    a) that

    b) to the doctor

    c) goes

1310. Choose the wrong word: "She is looking forward to go to Europe after she finishes her studies at the university.".

    a) looking

    b) go

    c) finishes

1311. Choose the wrong word: "Montaigne, the illustrious French philosophy, was elected mayor of Bordeaux, which was his home town.".

    a) philosophy

    b) was elected

    c) which was

1312. Choose the wrong word: "Certain pollens are more likely to cause an allergic reaction than another.".

    a) likely

    b) Certain

    c) another

1313. Choose the wrong word: "Computers have made access to information instantly available just by push a few buttons.".

    a) by push

    b) access

    c) have

1314. Choose the wrong word: "Mined over 1,000 years ago, gold is one of the earliest know metals."

    a) know

    b) the

    c) ago

1315. Choose the wrong word: "Many of the early world of T.S. Eliot expresses the anguish and barrenness of modern life and the isolation of the individual.".

    a) isolation

    b) Many

    c) expresses

1316. Choose the wrong word: "The novel reveal the horror, drudgery and joy of black life in rural Georgia.".

    a) The novel

    b) joy of

    c) reveal

1317. Choose the wrong word: "During wedding ceremonies in the US, guests are usually silence.".

    a) silence

    b) During

    c) guests

1318. Choose the wrong word: "How the Earth is in the shadow of the moon, we see an eclipse of the sun.".

    a) in the shadow

b) How

c) an

1319. Choose the wrong word: "The children's television program called Sesame Street was seeing in 84 countries.".

    a) The children's

    b) countries

    c) seeing

1320. Choose the wrong word: "Some research suggests what there is a link between the body's calcium balance and tooth decay.".

    a) what

    b) link between

    c) and

1321. Choose the wrong word: "To putting a large amount of information on a map, a variety of symbols must be used.".

    a) on

    b) variety

    c) To putting

1322. Choose the wrong word: "Before the nineteenth century it was rarely to find organized systems of adult education.".

    a) Before

    b) rarely

    c) systems

1323. Choose the wrong word: "Smoking is the number one prevent cause of death in the US.".

    a) prevent

    b) of death

    c) Smoking

1324. Choose the wrong word: "Not single alphabet has ever perfectly represented the sounds of any of Earth's natural languages.".

    a) sounds

    b) any of

    c) Not

1325. Choose the wrong word: "The ozone layer must be protected because it shield the Earth from excessive ultraviolet radiate.".

    a) radiate

    b) must be protected

    c) from

1326. Choose the wrong word: "Carbohydrates and fats are two essential sources of energy for animal grow.".

    a) and fats

    b) grow

    c) for

1327. Choose the wrong word: "By passing sunlight through a prism, the light is separate into a spectrum of colors.".

    a) through

    b) spectrum of

    c) is separate

1328. Choose the wrong word: "In spite modern medical technology, many diseases caused by viruses are still not curable.".

    a) In spite

    b) many

    c) by viruses

1329. Choose the wrong word: "Though Pablo Picasso was primarily a painting, he also became fine sculptor, engraver and ceramist.".

    a) fine

    b) painting

    c) primarily

1330. Choose the wrong word: "People who live in small towns often seem more warm and friendly than people who live in populated densely areas.".

    a) populated densely

    b) small towns

    c) who

1331. Choose the wrong word: "After visiting the museum he had not very much time left.".

    a) visiting

b) had not

c) very

1332. Choose the wrong word: "Before they had gone out they had been watching the news on TV.".

    a) had gone

    b) Before

    c) on

1333. Choose the wrong word: "She never wrote a letter by hand since she bought a word processor.".

    a) by

    b) since

    c) wrote

1334. Choose the wrong word: "Please promise not telling anybody my secret.".

    a) promise

    b) telling

    c) not

1335. Choose the wrong word: "Maria had never complained about have a handicap.".

    a) have

    b) complained

    c) about

1336. Choose the wrong word: "I enjoy to talk to her on the phone. I look forward to seeing her next week.".

    a) look

    b) to seeing

    c) to talk

1337. Choose the wrong word: "When I entered the room, I saw my young son to stand on the kitchen table.".

    a) saw

    b) to stand on

    c) young

1338. Choose the wrong word: "Mr. Smith didn't remember bring his passport when he went to the consulate.".
  a) went
  b) bring
  c) to

1339. Choose the wrong word: "George hasn't completed the assignment yet and Mary hasn't neither.".
  a) hasn't neither
  b) yet
  c) has not

1340. Choose the wrong word: "After Steve eaten dinner, he wrote several letters and went to bed.".
  a) he wrote
  b) several letters
  c) eaten

1341. Choose the wrong word: "After she had bought himself a new automobile, she sold her bicycle.".
  a) she sold
  b) himself
  c) her

1342. Choose the wrong word: "He was drink a cup of coffee when the telephone rang.".
  a) was drink
  b) a cup
  c) when

1343. Choose the wrong word: "When you come after class this afternoon, we discussed the possibility of your writing a research paper.".
  a) When
  b) after
  c) discussed

1344. Choose the wrong word: "A short time before her operation last month, Mrs. Smith dreams of her daughter who lives overseas.".
  a) dreams

b) last

c) A short time

1345. Choose the wrong word: "After she had dressed and ate breakfast, Sarah rushed off to her office for a meeting with her accountant.".

    a) to her

    b) ate

    c) with

1346. Choose the wrong word: "The teacher repeated the assignment again for the students, since they had difficulty understanding what to do.".

    a) The teacher

    b) again

    c) since they

1347. Choose the wrong word: "The company has little money that it can't hardly operate anymore.".

    a) has

    b) that it

    c) little

1348. Choose the wrong word: "The professor is thinking to go to the conference on environment next month.".

    a) next month

    b) to go

    c) is

1349. Choose the wrong word: "The statement will be spoken just one time; therefore, you must listen very careful.".

    a) will be spoken

    b) must listen

    c) careful

1350. Choose the wrong word: "The pilot agreed to land the plane only when the hijackers threatened to shoot some of the passenger.".

    a) passenger

    b) to land

    c) only

1351. Choose the wrong word: "Someone was showed the child how to use the telephone.".

    a) to use

    b) was showed

    c) the

1352. Choose the wrong word: "The search party had idea little where start looking.".

    a) had

    b) looking

    c) idea little

1353. Choose the wrong word: "Police have to break the meeting up yesterday.".

    a) have to

    b) break

    c) the

1354. Choose the wrong word: "We are suppose to read all of chapter seven and answer the question for tomorrow's class.".

    a) suppose

    b) all of chapter

    c) answer

1355. Choose the wrong word: "Because the committee was anxious to attend the celebration, the president dispensed to reading the minutes.".

    a) the

    b) minutes

    c) to reading

1356. Choose the wrong word: "The customer was interested see one of those new pocket cameras with the built-in flash.".

    a) those

    b) see

    c) the built-in

1357. Choose the wrong word: "My teacher said we should write another composition for tomorrow related for our experience at last week's workshop.".

    a) related for

b) should write

c) at

1358. Choose the wrong word: "The jury be trying to reach a decision.".

    a) The

    b) reach

    c) be

1359. Choose the wrong word: "Of the two landscape that you have shown me, this one is the more picturesque.".

    a) that

    b) Of the two landscape

    c) the more

1360. Choose the wrong word: "Daniel didn't lose any time in applying for the teaching position on math.".

    a) on math

    b) lose

    c) in applying

1361. Choose the wrong word: "When the roads became too slippery, we decided to return to the cabin and wait for the storm to subsiding.".

    a) too slippery

    b) to return

    c) subsiding

1362. Choose the wrong word: "When teenagers finish high school, they have several choices; going to college, getting a job or the army.".

    a) teenagers

    b) the army

    c) going to

1363. Choose the wrong word: "Teachers whom do not spend enough time on class preparation often have difficulty in explaining new lessons.".

    a) enough time

    b) whom

    c) class preparation

1364. Choose the wrong word: "The hotel was such very noise that they couldn't sleep.".

a) such very noise

b) couldn't sleep

c) The hotel

1365. Choose the wrong word: "Get on the bus outside the station and get them off at Park street.".

    a) Get on

    b) outside

    c) get them off

1366. Choose the wrong word: "We were married for twenty-five years, Helen. You could at least give me a chance to run.".

    a) were married

    b) at least

    c) chance

1367. Choose the wrong word: "Their room had such a very unpleasant view that it makes them feel quite miserable.".

    a) Their room

    b) it makes

    c) such

1368. Choose the wrong word: "I don't know why she talks in so a loud voice.".

    a) I don't know

    b) she talks

    c) so

1369. Choose the wrong word: "Because it was a long time since I knew him I am not sure if I will remember him.".

    a) was

    b) sure if

    c) a long time

1370. Choose the wrong word: "Colonists used an extensive system of barter in order to a lack of money and credit might be overcome.".

    a) Colonists

    b) in order to

    c) might be

1371. Choose the wrong word: "We are going to stop here for a moment to get some petrols.".

    a) petrols

    b) here

    c) for a moment

1372. Choose the wrong word: "One way to save words is by using infinitive phrase instead to clauses.".

    a) One way

    b) using infinitive

    c) instead to

1373. Choose the wrong word: "The headquarters can be found in Black Street in California.".

    a) in

    b) can be found

    c) headquarters

1374. Choose the wrong word: "If a small child plays with matches, he or she might get burnt.".

    a) small child

    b) might

    c) plays with

1375. Choose the wrong word: "Is finish a job you have started very important to you?".

    a) to you

    b) finish

    c) have started

1376. Choose the wrong word: "Not smoking and drinking alcohol are the most important things you can do talking care of your health.".

    a) your health

    b) Not

    c) talking care

1377. Choose the wrong word: "Gunpowder, is some ways the most effective of all the explosive materials, were a mixture of potassium nitrate, charcoal and sulfur.".

    a) all the

b) were

c) of

1378. Choose the wrong word: "What should you do if you've finish to use your calculator?".

      a) to use

      b) should

      c) if

1379. Choose the wrong word: "Travelling to a foreign country is always interesting, especially if it is a country that is completely different to your own.".

      a) is completely

      b) always interesting

      c) different to

1380. Choose the wrong word: "It is generally a best idea to place the thesis statement at or near the end of the introductory paragraph.".

      a) best idea

      b) place

      c) at or near

1381. Choose the wrong word: "There are many similarities and differences among life in the country and life in the city.".

      a) There are

      b) among

      c) life

1382. Choose the wrong word: "My friends are still talking about the day while I fell in the river.".

      a) are

      b) while

      c) fell in

1383. Choose the wrong word: "Daniel found himself in a room where was very large and dark.".

      a) where

      b) large

      c) dark

1384. Choose the wrong word: "She stopped to write her letter because she had to leave for school.".
- a) because
- b) for school
- c) to write

1385. Choose the wrong word: "Sarah is finally used to cook on electric stove.".
- a) is
- b) to cook
- c) finally

1386. Choose the wrong word: "They are going to have to leave soon and so do we.".
- a) so do
- b) to have to
- c) leave soon

1387. Choose the wrong word: "How much times did they have to do the experiment?".
- a) have to
- b) times
- c) How much

1388. Choose the wrong word: "She refused to tell us why was she crying.".
- a) was she crying
- b) refused
- c) to tell

1389. Choose the wrong word: "A lunch of soup and sandwiches do not appeal to all of the students.".
- a) of soup
- b) appeal to all
- c) do not

1390. Choose the wrong word: "Mrs. Johnson, along with her cousins from Spain, are planning to attend the festivities.".
- a) to attend

b) are

c) with her

1391. Choose the wrong word: "When you get burns, you should ease the pain with warmly water packs.".

    a) warmly

    b) burns

    c) should

1392. Choose the wrong word: "The shop cross the road is where I bought the flowers from.".

    a) where

    b) the flowers from

    c) cross the road

1393. Choose the wrong word: "It was really surprise that those children survived the fire that destroyed all the houses.".

    a) those

    b) It was really surprise

    c) survived

1394. Choose the wrong word: "She was afraid that the English teacher would be angry to her because she left her book at home.".

    a) to

    b) was afraid

    c) left

1395. Choose the wrong word: "If you try to concentrate on one subject for too long, you might fed-up and not really learn anything.".

    a) to concentrate

    b) on

    c) might fed-up

1396. Choose the wrong word: "Silk used to rank first between our crops, but it represents only a fraction of the production now.".

    a) between

    b) rank

    c) represents

1397. Choose the wrong word: "Salmon live in salt water when most of their adult lives.".

    a) in salt water

    b) when

    c) lives

1398. Choose the wrong word: "To building their nests, these birds use their bills as needles.".

    a) nests

    b) as

    c) building

1399. Choose the wrong word: "Fountain pens first became commercial available about a hundred years ago.".

    a) first

    b) commercial

    c) about

1400. Choose the wrong word: "With its strong claws and its many protruding tooth a gopher is an excellent digger.".

    a) protruding tooth

    b) strong claws

    c) With

Answers

1.a	2.b	3.c	4.a	5.b	6.c	7.a	8.b	9.a	10.c
11.c	12.a	13.b	14.c	15.b	16.c	17.a	18.b	19.c	20.b
21.b	22.c	23.a	24.b	25.a	26.c	27.b	28.a	29.c	30.a
31.b	32.c	33.a	34.c	35.b	36.b	37.b	38.a	39.c	40.a
41.b	42.a	43.c	44.a	45.c	46.b	47.a	48.c	49.c	50.b
51.a	52.c	53.a	54.b	55.c	56.b	57.b	58.c	59.a	60.c
61.c	62.a	63.b	64.c	65.a	66.b	67.c	68.c	69.b	70.a
71.c	72.c	73.b	74.a	75.c	76.c	77.b	78.a	79.c	80.b
81.b	82.c	83.a	84.c	85.b	86.a	87.c	88.c	89.b	90.a
91.c	92.a	93.b	94.c	95.a	96.b	97.c	98.a	99.b	100.c

101.a	102.b	103.c	104.a	105.b	106.c	107.a	108.c	109.b
110.a	111.b	112.a	113.c	114.a	115.b	116.c	117.c	118.a
119.b	120.c	121.b	122.c	123.a	124.c	125.b	126.b	127.c
128.c	129.a	130.b	131.a	132.c	133.c	134.b	135.c	136.c
137.a	138.b	139.c	140.a	141.a	142.c	143.b	144.c	145.a
146.c	147.c	148.b	149.a	150.b	151.c	152.c	153.a	154.b
155.c	156.a	157.b	158.c	159.c	160.b	161.b	162.a	163.c
164.c	165.b	166.a	167.c	168.b	169.a	170.c	171.c	172.a
173.c	174.b	175.c	176.a	177.b	178.b	179.a	180.c	181.a
182.c	183.b	184.a	185.c	186.b	187.c	188.a	189.b	190.c
191.c	192.a	193.b	194.c	195.b	196.a	197.c	198.c	199.b
200.a	201.b	202.c	203.b	204.a	205.c	206.a	207.c	208.b
209.a	210.c	211.c	212.c	213.a	214.b	215.c	216.b	217.a
218.c	219.b	220.a	221.c	222.b	223.a	224.c	225.a	226.b
227.b	228.c	229.b	230.a	231.c	232.a	233.b	234.c	235.a
236.b	237.c	238.c	239.b	240.a	241.b	242.c	243.c	244.b
245.a	246.a	247.b	248.c	249.b	250.a	251.a	252.c	253.b
254.a	255.c	256.b	257.a	258.c	259.b	260.a	261.c	262.a
263.c	264.b	265.b	266.a	267.c	268.a	269.b	270.c	271.b
272.a	273.c	274.b	275.a	276.b	277.c	278.a	279.b	280.c
281.c	282.a	283.b	284.a	285.c	286.c	287.a	288.b	289.c
290.a	291.b	292.c	293.a	294.c	295.a	296.b	297.b	298.c
299.a	300.b	301.c	302.a	303.b	304.b	305.a	306.b	307.c
308.b	309.a	310.c	311.c	312.a	313.a	314.c	315.b	316.c
317.b	318.a	319.c	320.b	321.a	322.a	323.c	324.a	325.b
326.a	327.c	328.b	329.b	330.a	331.a	332.b	333.b	334.c
335.a	336.c	337.b	338.c	339.a	340.c	341.b	342.a	343.c
344.a	345.b	346.a	347.c	348.a	349.c	350.b	351.b	352.c
353.a	354.c	355.b	356.a	357.c	358.c	359.a	360.c	361.b
362.a	363.b	364.c	365.a	366.c	367.b	368.a	369.c	370.c
371.b	372.a	373.c	374.b	375.c	376.a	377.c	378.b	379.a
380.c	381.c	382.b	383.a	384.c	385.b	386.c	387.a	388.b
389.c	390.a	391.a	392.c	393.c	394.b	394.b	395.b	396.a
397.c	398.c	399.b	400.a	401.b	402.c	403.a	404.c	405.c
406.a	407.b	408.b	409.a	410.c	411.a	412.c	413.b	414.a

415.c	416.c	417.a	418.b	419.c	420.a	421.b	422.c	423.a
424.b	425.c	426.a	427.b	428.a	429.c	430.b	431.a	432.c

433.a	434.b	435.c	436.b	437.c	438.a	439.b	440.c	441.a
442.c	443.b	444.a	445.c	446.a	447.b	448.c	449.a	450.b
451.a	452.b	453.c	454.a	455.b	456.a	457.c	458.c	459.b
460.c	461.c	462.b	463.a	464.b	465.c	466.a	467.b	468.a
469.c	470.c	471.c	472.a	473.b	474.a	475.b	476.c	477.a
478.a	479.b	480.c	472.a	482.c	483.a	484.b	485.c	486.b
487.a	488.b	489.b	490.a	491.c	492.a	493.b	494.c	495.b
496.c	497.a	498.c	499.b	500.a	501.a	502.c	503.b	504.b
505.c	506.a	507.b	508.c	509.a	510.b	511.c	512.a	513.b
514.c	515.a	516.b	517.b	518.a	519.c	520.b	521.c	522.c
523.b	524.a	525.c	526.c	527.b	528.c	529.a	530.b	531.a
532.c	533.b	534.c	535.a	536.c	537.a	538.c	539.b	540.a
541.c	542.b	543.a	544.b	545.c	546.b	547.a	548.a	549.c
550.b	551.c	552.a	553.a	554.b	555.a	556.c	557.b	558.a
559.a	560.b	561.b	562.c	563.a	564.c	565.a	566.b	567.c
568.c	569.a	570.b	571.c	572.a	573.b	574.c	575.a	576.b
577.c	578.c	579.b	580.a	581.b	582.a	583.c	584.b	585.b
586.a	587.c	588.a	589.b	590.b	591.c	592.a	593.b	594.c
595.a	596.b	597.c	598.a	599.b	600.c	601.a	602.c	603.b
604.b	605.a	606.c	607.a	608.c	609.c	610.a	611.c	612.b
613.a	614.b	615.c	616.b	617.b	618.a	619.c	620.a	621.b
622.c	623.a	624.b	625.c	626.b	627.a	628.b	629.b	630.a
631.c	632.b	633.a	634.c	635.b	636.a	637.c	638.a	639.b
640.c	641.b	642.a	643.c	644.a	645.b	646.c	647.a	648.b
649.a	650.c	651.c	652.c	653.a	654.b	655.a	656.a	657.c
658.b	659.a	660.c	661.c	662.a	663.b	664.c	665.b	666.c
667.b	668.a	669.c	670.a	671.a	672.b	673.c	674.a	675.a
676.b	677.c	678.b	679.a	680.c	681.a	682.c	683.b	684.a
685.c	686.b	687.a	688.c	689.b	690.a	691.c	692.a	693.b
694.a	695.c	696.a	697.c	698.c	699.b	700.a	701.c	702.a
703.b	704.a	705.c	706.a	707.b	708.b	709.c	710.a	711.b
712.c	713.a	714.c	715.a	716.b	717.b	718.c	719.a	720.b
721.a	722.b	723.c	724.b	725.a	726.a	727.c	728.b	729.b
730.a	731.c	732.c	733.b	734.b	735.a	736.b	737.c	738.b
739.c	740.b	741.a	742.a	743.c	744.c	745.b	746.c	747.a
748.b	749.c	750.a	751.b	752.a	753.c	754.b	755.a	756.c
757.c	758.b	759.a	760.c	761.a	762.b	763.c	764.a	765.c
766.b	767.c	768.a	769.c	770.a	771.b	772.c	773.b	774.a
775.c	776.c	777.a	778.b	779.b	780.c	781.a	782.c	783.b
784.a	785.c	786.a	787.b	788.c	789.b	790.a	791.b	792.c

793.a	794.c	795.a	796.b	797.c	798.c	799.b	800.a	801.c
802.a	803.a	804.b	805.c	806.b	807.c	808.b	809.a	810.a
811.c	812.a	813.c	814.b	815.a	816.b	817.c	818.a	819.b
820.c	821.c	822.b	823.a	824.b	825.a	826.c	827.b	828.c
829.a	830.c	831.c	832.a	833.c	834.b	835.c	836.a	837.b
838.a	839.c	840.b	841.b	842.a	843.c	844.b	845.b	846.a
847.c	848.b	849.c	850.a	851.c	852.b	853.b	854.c	855.a
856.b	857.a	858.c	859.b	860.a	861.c	862.b	863.a	864.c
865.a	866.b	867.a	868.a	869.c	870.a	871.b	872.c	873.c
874.a	875.b	876.a	877.c	878.b	879.a	880.c	881.c	882.a
883.b	884.c	885.b	886.a	887.b	888.c	889.a	890.b	891.c

892.a	893.b	894.a	895.b	896.c	897.b	898.b	899.a	900.a
901.c	902.b	903.c	904.a	905.a	906.b	907.a	908.c	909.b
910.a	911.a	912.c	913.c	914.b	915.c	916.b	917.a	918.b
919.c	920.a	921.b	922.c	923.b	924.a	925.c	926.b	927.a
928.c	929.a	930.b	931.c	932.b	933.a	934.a	935.c	936.b
937.a	938.c	939.c	940.b	941.b	942.a	943.c	944.b	945.a
946.c	947.b	948.b	949.a	950.c	951.a	952.b	953.c	954.a
955.b	956.c	957.a	958.b	959.c	960.a	961.c	962.b	963.a
964.c	965.b	966.a	967.b	968.a	969.c	970.a	971.b	972.c
973.a	974.b	975.c	976.b	977.a	978.b	979.c	980.a	981.c
982.b	983.a	984.c	985.b	986.c	987.a	988.b	989.c	990.b
991.c	992.a	993.b	994.a	995.b	996.a	997.c	998.b	999.a
1000.c	1001.c	1002.a	1003.b	1004.c	1005.a	1006.a	1007.c	1008.a
1009.b	1010.b	1011.b	1012.a	1013.c	1014.b	1015.a	1016.c	1017.b
1018.a	1019.a	1020.c	1021.b	1022.a	1023.b	1024.a	1025.c	1026.c
1027.a	1028.b	1029.c	1030.a	1031.c	1032.b	1033.b	1034.c	1035.a
1036.c	1037.b	1038.a	1039.b	1040.c	1041.c	1042.a	1043.b	1044.a
1045.c	1046.b	1047.a	1048.b	1049.c	1050.b	1051.a	1052.c	1053.a
1054.b	1055.a	1056.b	1057.c	1058.b	1059.b	1060.a	1061.a	1062.c
1063.b	1064.a	1065.b	1066.c	1067.b	1068.c	1069.a	1070.b	1071.a
1072.c	1073.b	1074.a	1075.b	1076.b	1077.c	1078.a	1079.b	1080.c
1081.a	1082.c	1083.a	1084.b	1085.b	1086.c	1087.a	1088.b	1089.c
1090.a	1091.c	1092.c	1093.a	1094.b	1095.c	1096.a	1097.b	1098.a
1099.c	1100.a	1101.b	1102.b	1103.a	1104.c	1105.c	1106.b	1107.a
1108.c	1109.b	1110.a	1111.c	1112.b	1113.a	1114.c	1115.a	1116.c
1117.b	1118.c	1119.a	1120.c	1121.c	1122.b	1123.a	1124.c	1125.a

1126.b	1127.b	1128.c	1129.a	1130.b	1131.c	1132.a	1133.b	1134.b
1135.c	1136.b	1137.a	1138.c	1139.a	1140.b	1141.c	1142.a	1143.b
1144.b	1145.a	1146.c	1147.b	1148.b	1149.a	1150.c	1151.b	1152.a
1153.c	1154.b	1155.c	1156.a	1157.c	1158.a	1159.b	1160.b	1161.a
1162.c	1163.b	1164.a	1165.c	1166.a	1167.a	1168.c	1169.b	1170.a
1171.a	1172.c	1173.b	1174.b	1175.a	1176.c	1177.c	1178.a	1179.b
1180.c	1181.a	1182.b	1183.c	1184.c	1185.a	1186.b	1187.a	1188.b
1189.c	1190.a	1191.c	1192.a	1193.b	1194.a	1195.c	1196.a	1197.b
1198.a	1199.c	1200.a	1201.b	1202.c	1203.a	1204.b	1205.c	1206.a
1207.b	1208.c	1209.a	1210.b	1211.c	1212.b	1213.a	1214.a	1215.c
1216.a	1217.b	1218.c	1219.c	1220.a	1221.b	1222.c	1223.a	1224.b
1225.a	1226.c	1227.c	1228.b	1229.c	1230.a	1231.b	1232.c	1233.a
1234.c	1235.b	1236.a	1237.b	1238.c	1239.a	1240.b	1241.c	1242.a
1243.b	1244.a	1245.c	1246.c	1247.a	1248.b	1249.a	1250.c	1251.c
1252.b	1253.c	1254.a	1255.b	1256.a	1257.c	1258.b	1259.b	1260.a
1261.b	1262.a	1263.b	1264.c	1265.b	1266.a	1267.b	1268.c	1269.b
1270.c	1271.c	1272.a	1273.c	1274.b	1275.b	1276.a	1277.c	1278.b
1279.c	1280.a	1281.c	1282.c	1283.b	1284.c	1285.c	1286.b	1287.a
1288.b	1289.c	1290.b	1291.a	1292.b	1293.c	1294.b	1295.a	1296.b
1297.c	1298.a	1299.b	1300.c	1301.a	1302.c	1303.c	1304.c	1305.b

1306.b	1307.c	1308.a	1309.c	1310.b	1311.a	1312.c	1313.a	1314.a
1315.b	1316.c	1317.a	1318.b	1319.c	1320.a	1321.c	1322.b	1323.a
1324.c	1325.a	1326.b	1327.c	1328.a	1329.b	1330.a	1331.b	1332.a
1333.c	1334.b	1335.a	1336.c	1337.b	1338.b	1339.a	1340.c	1341.b

1342.a	1343.c	1344.a	1345.b	1346.b	1347.c	1348.b	1349.c	1350.a
1351.b	1352.c	1353.a	1354.a	1355.c	1356.b	1357.a	1358.c	1359.b
1360.a	1361.c	1362.b	1363.b	1364.a	1365.c	1366.a	1367.b	1368.c
1369.a	1370.b	1371.a	1372.c	1373.a	1374.b	1375.b	1376.c	1377.b
1378.a	1379.c	1380.a	1381.b	1382.b	1383.a	1384.c	1385.b	1386.a
1387.c	1388.a	1389.c	1390.b	1391.a	1392.c	1393.b	1394.a	1395.c
1396.a	1397.b	1398.c	1399.b	1400.a				

Conclusion

In conclusion I want to thank you for buying my book and I hope you find it useful. Please pay attention to further personally crafted English Grammar books which I intend to release.

Take care and good luck!

Write a review

I am constantly improving my books and my work, trying to deliver to my readers the best quality information. To improve my work and myself as a human being, I need organic reviews to know where I am wrong or where I have made mistakes. Remember, there is no such thing as a perfect book, it needs updates all the time, especially if it's digital. If this book has been useful to you, please, write a review with all your thoughts. It won't take more than 1 minute. If you didn't like something from this book, please contact me and I will try to solve your problem.

Honestly,

Daniel B. Smith

Manufactured by Amazon.ca
Acheson, AB

11179678R00125